The Adams

L. H. BUTTERFIELD, EDIT

SERIES I

DIARIES

Diary and Auto
of John A

SUPPLEME

The Earliest Diary
of John Adams

L. H. BUTTERFIELD, *EDITOR*

WENDELL D. GARRETT AND MARC FRIEDLAENDER
ASSOCIATE EDITORS

—————————— ☆ ——————————

June 1753–April 1754
September 1758–January 1759

THE BELKNAP PRESS
OF HARVARD UNIVERSITY PRESS
CAMBRIDGE, MASSACHUSETTS

1966

Distributed in Great Britain by Oxford University Press · London

Funds for editing *The Adams Papers* have been provided by Time, Inc., on behalf of *Life,* and by the Ford Foundation, to the Massachusetts Historical Society, under whose supervision the editorial work is being done.

Library of Congress Catalog Card Number 66-14442 · Printed in the United States of America

This edition of *The Adams Papers*
is sponsored by the MASSACHUSETTS HISTORICAL SOCIETY
to which the ADAMS MANUSCRIPT TRUST
by a deed of gift dated 4 April 1956
gave ultimate custody of the personal and public papers
written, accumulated, and preserved over a span of three centuries
by the Adams family of Massachusetts

The Adams Papers

ADMINISTRATIVE BOARD

EDITORIAL ADVISORY COMMITTEE

The acorn and oakleaf device on the preceding page is redrawn from a seal cut for John Quincy Adams after 1830. The motto is from Cæcilius Statius as quoted by Cicero in the First Tusculan Disputation: *Serit arbores quæ alteri seculo prosint* ("He plants trees for the benefit of later generations").

Contents

Descriptive List of Illustrations

The illustrations are between pages 42 and 43. Those not otherwise attributed are from the Royall Tyler Collection, Gift of Helen Tyler Brown, courtesy of the Vermont Historical Society. Pages cited in ornamental brackets (⁅ ⁆) refer to the (editorially supplied) pagination of the MS.

1. FIRST PAGE OF JOHN ADAMS' EARLIEST DIARY, JUNE 1753

Written when he was seventeen and beginning his third year at Harvard, this page not only initiated Adams' long series of diaries, but is the earliest example of his handwriting now known. Although in the large and rather round hand that, later on, he tended to reserve for formal rather than personal purposes, the general cast of the writing makes it immediately recognizable as Adams'. Compare, on the one hand, page ⁅ 9 ⁆ of the MS (illustrated below), which shows Adams experimenting the next year with a different style of penmanship, and, on the other, with the small hand of pages ⁅ 15 ⁆ and ⁅ 23 ⁆ of the MS (also illustrated below), written in 1758, when his writing had matured in almost all respects.

The variations in the handwriting found in Adams' *Earliest Diary* are discussed in the Introduction at p. 8–9. The impulses that led to his keeping this first diary are discussed at p. 33–34.

2. PROFESSOR WINTHROP'S NOTES FOR HIS "COURSE OF... LECTURES" IN NATURAL PHILOSOPHY AT HARVARD

Elected "Hollisian Professor of the Mathematicks and of natural and Experimental Philosophy" in 1738, John Winthrop prepared in 1746 a "Summary of a Course Of Experimental Philosophical Lectures" in MS, of which a flyleaf and the first three pages of text, including the whole of his notes for "Lecture 1st.," on Motion, are reproduced here. There were thirty-three lectures in the full "Course," but in 1754, when John Adams attended and took notes on the lectures (see the following illustration), only eight were delivered, for the reason given in a note on the entry of 11 April 1754, p. 64, below.

Professor Winthrop's "lecture hall and laboratory was the western room of the second story of Old Harvard, and he made it a place of significance in the history of science in America" (Sibley-Shipton, *Harvard Graduates*, 9:244). His influence on young John Adams

was more profound and lasting than that of any other member of
the Harvard faculty; see the Introduction at p. 34–35.
Courtesy of the Harvard University Archives.

3. NOTES, IN ADAMS' VARIANT HAND, ON WINTHROP'S FIRST LECTURE, I APRIL 1754

This page contains half of Adams' notes on Professor Winthrop's
first lecture, treating of Motion; see the preceding illustration for
Winthrop's own notes for the same lecture. As engaging as anything
else in this undergraduate journal is Adams' confession that, although Winthrop had explained to the class the laws to which
"motion is subject," Adams had "forgot" them.

Like many undergraduates before and since, Adams experimented
with his handwriting. Except for the caption-date and an occasional
letter or word in the text, this page ⊰ 9 ⊱, if seen independently,
could scarcely be identified as in Adams' hand. Compare the first
page of the MS, written in 1753, illustrated above, and two later
pages ⊰ 15, 23 ⊱, written in 1758, illustrated below; also the discussion in the Introduction at p. 8–9.

4. PROFESSOR JOHN WINTHROP, ABOUT 1773, BY JOHN SINGLETON COPLEY

Although he was a versatile scientist, John Winthrop (1714–
1779), A.B. Harvard 1732, LL.D. Edinburgh 1771 and Harvard
1773, F.R.S., probably made his most valuable contributions as an
astronomer and thus initiated Harvard's distinction as a center of
astronomical research. In 1761, for example, Winthrop took a
voyage to Newfoundland, accompanied by two student assistants,
to observe the transit of Venus, a principal purpose of which was to
determine the distance of the earth from the sun. The Harvard
Corporation voted to pay the expenses of this earliest scientific
expedition sponsored by an American educational institution, and
allowed Winthrop to borrow such apparatus owned by the College
as would be useful to him.

It was therefore appropriate that Copley in this striking portrait
chose to represent John Adams' favorite teacher seated beside his
telescope. The window, the landscape, and the heavens upon which
the instrument is trained are conventionalized in the manner of the
day; the setting might be either Harvard Hall or Winthrop's house
on the northwest corner of present Boylston and Mount Auburn
streets. But the telescope itself is a good representation of a reflector
telescope made by the well-known James Short of London which
belonged to Winthrop personally and is still extant. It was given to
Harvard after its owner's death and is permanently exhibited in the
library at Winthrop House beneath the portrait in which it figures.

See the note on Winthrop at p. 46, below. See also I. Bernard
Cohen, *Some Early Tools of American Science* . . . , Cambridge,

1950, p. 37–39; Brooke Hindle, *The Pursuit of Science in Revolutionary America, 1735–1789*, Chapel Hill, 1956, p. 99–100. Information on Winthrop's telescope now in Winthrop House has been kindly furnished to the editors by Mr. David P. Wheatland.

Concerning the portrait, see Barbara Neville Parker and Anne Bolling Wheeler, *John Singleton Copley: American Portraits*, Boston, 1938, p. 209–210; Jules D. Prown, *John Singleton Copley* (in press 1965).

Courtesy of Harvard University.

5. SAMUEL QUINCY, ABOUT 1767, BY JOHN SINGLETON COPLEY

"How resolutely, how inviolably, how surprizingly we have preserv'd and pursued The Resolution of writing each other upon Points of Law, which we took at Weighmouth," John Adams wrote to his friend Sam Quincy late in 1758 (draft at p. 66, below). But this was pure sarcasm, for nothing had followed the vow the two young law students had taken some time before. Samuel Quincy (1734–1789), brother of the "Orlinda" (Hannah Quincy) of the present diary, had graduated at Harvard a year ahead of Adams, trained for the law in the Boston office of Benjamin Prat, and was admitted to the Suffolk bar on the same day with Adams in November 1758. Adams was long and deeply attached to Quincy, a convivial man as well as an able practitioner. But in 1771 Quincy accepted appointment under the crown as solicitor general and a secret retainer from the tea-tax revenue, and, as the Revolution approached, broke with his family on the great political issue of the day, left for England in May 1775, and never returned to Massachusetts, though he longed to. See the note on Quincy at p. 68, below, and references there; see also JA, *Legal Papers*, 1:cvii–cviii, and numerous references in its index to cases in which Adams and Quincy were engaged as colleagues or opponents.

On this portrait of Quincy in his barrister's gown, see Barbara Neville Parker and Anne Bolling Wheeler, *John Singleton Copley: American Portraits*, Boston, 1938, p. 158–159; Jules D. Prown, *John Singleton Copley* (in press 1965).

Courtesy of Miss Grace W. Treadwell, on loan to the Museum of Fine Arts, Boston.

6. JOHN ADAMS' SCIENTIFIC MANUAL AT HARVARD: NIEUWENTIJDT'S "RELIGIOUS PHILOSOPHER"

As an undergraduate, Adams supplemented Professor Winthrop's lectures and laboratory experiments with reading in this popular and handsomely illustrated compilation of scientific "Discoveries," "Laws," and "Demonstrations" by the learned mathematician and physician Bernard Nieuwentijdt (1654–1718), of Purmerende in Holland. See entry of 20 June 1753 and notes, p. 45–46, below. Originally published at Amsterdam in 1714 under the title *Het Regt Gebruik der Werelt Beschouwingen* ("The Right Use of the

Contemplation of the World"), and first issued in English in London four years later, Nieuwentijdt's book, "designed for the Conviction of Atheists and Infidels," exhibited an ardently teleological view of the world and its creatures as then known. It was thus highly acceptable to readers in both Europe and America in the 18th century, and copies in French and English as well as in Dutch are commonly listed in private and institutional libraries of the period. No Adams copy has been found; this copy of a mixed third and fourth edition, 3 vols., London, 1730, was acquired in 1733 by Samuel Cooke, Harvard 1735.

Courtesy of the Boston Athenæum.

7. THE GRIDLEY-ADAMS COPY OF VAN MUYDEN'S ABRIDGMENT OF JUSTINIAN'S "INSTITUTES"

When John Adams, fresh from his legal apprenticeship in Worcester, called in the fall of 1758 on the great Boston lawyer Jeremy Gridley to seek advice and help in gaining admission to the bar, Gridley wanted to know not only what common-law books the younger man had read, but what works in Roman or civil law as well. The fact that Adams had read any civil law at all impressed Gridley, and, Adams remembered, "He lead me up a pair of Stairs into a Chamber in which he had a very handsome library of the civil and Cannon Laws and Writers in the Law of Nature and Nations. Shewing me a Number of small manuals and Compendiums of the civil Law he put one of them into my hand, and said put that in your Pocket and when you return that I will lend you any other you cho[o]se" (*Diary and Autobiography*, 3:271). The book Adams put in his pocket was undoubtedly the very copy of Van Muyden's small *Tractatio* on Justinian's famous *Institutes* here illustrated, for on 26 October he recorded the loan in his *Diary* (same, 1:56). In December he was still creeping through the Dutch commentator's crabbed Latin (same, p. 63). The very untidy notes on the *Tractatio* that he entered at two different places in his *Earliest Diary* were probably written in December 1758 or early 1759; see p. 55–59, 100–101, below.

Johannes van Muyden (1652?–1729), of Utrecht, was one of the great Dutch school of commentators on the civil law. The first edition of this *Tractatio*, one of a number he published, was issued at Utrecht in 1694. See *Nieuw Ned. Biog. Woordenboek*, 2:969.

For Adams' studies in, and use of, civil law, see his *Legal Papers*, 1:lv–lvi, lxxiv–lxxv, and its index under "Civil law."

From the three signatures on the titlepage and other available evidence, one may guess that this copy of Van Muyden was first owned by "Jo: Campbell" (not further identified) and then by "Jer. Gridley"; that it was returned in due time by Adams to its owner; and that Adams purchased it (with other books known to have come from the same source) at the sale of Gridley's library after his death in 1767.

Courtesy of the Boston Public Library.

8. DRAFT OF A LETTER FROM JOHN ADAMS TO SAMUEL QUINCY: "MY RESOLUTIONS ARE LIKE BUBBLES"

The present page ⊰ 15 ⊱ is typical (though above average in legibility) of the make-up of Adams' Diary Fragment (the MS of his *Earliest Diary*) after he returned to Braintree in October 1758. For the improvement of his style, he began drafting his letters to his friends in his old diary booklet. At the top of this page is the conclusion of a letter to Tristram Dalton. Then follows his letter to Samuel Quincy reminding him of their mutual but unfulfilled vow to correspond on "Points of Law." At the foot, upside down and presumably inserted later, is a scrap from Virgil applied to a number of Adams' young friends (including Sam Quincy) who are consumed by the secret fires of love. This may very well have been a warning to himself in connection with his current interest in Sam's sister Hannah ("Orlinda").

The hand is essentially Adams' small mature hand, familiar in his law notes, pocket diaries, and other personal writings for many years to come. Contrast the two earlier pages ⊰ 1, 9 ⊱ from the Diary Fragment reproduced in facsimile among these illustrations.

9. DRAFT OF A LETTER FROM JOHN ADAMS TO WILLIAM CRAWFORD: "YOU MUST NOT CONCLUDE...THAT I AM IN THE VAPOURS"

Another typical page, ⊰ 23 ⊱ in the MS, written late in 1758, in what had by now become for Adams an all-purpose miscellany rather than a diary. At the top is a query, which can be made out with effort, concerning Luke Lambert's horses that trampled Joseph Field's crops and led to Adams' first case as a trial lawyer. Then follows a draft letter, deliberately casual in tone, to his friend Crawford, inquiring about friends in Worcester and particularly about a girl there named Betsy Greene. The draft is initialed "J.A.," the only occurrence in the Diary Fragment of Adams' name in any form. Finally there are detached quotations and reflections on Fame and Reputation, matters of absorbing interest to an intensely ambitious young man making his start in the world.

10. JOHN ADAMS' BOOK OF SELECTED ORATIONS OF CICERO

This hard-used little book belonged to a long succession of schoolboys, three of whose names appear here, reflecting their ownership probably in this order: John Adams, who paid a pound (or a guinea) in Massachusetts currency for it early in 1750 when preparing for Harvard; Adams' classmate, William Whittemore, who may have used it as a freshman in college; and John Stevens, Harvard 1766. At some point thereafter it made its way back to Adams or his family, doubtless because Adams had written his name so boldly and frequently in the front leaves. On the first flyleaf, not shown here, he displayed his powers as a Latinist by adding below his name: "Hoc nomen pono quia hunc Librum perdere nolo."

Two presumably earlier owners' names also appear on this first fly-leaf, but they are illegible; and at the foot are three faintly penciled names all in the same hand (which cannot be certainly identified): "J Q Adams / G Adams / J Adams"—a son and two grandsons of the first Adams owner.

John Adams read Cicero at all stages of his life, and never with keener interest than in 1758 when, as an aspiring advocate, he analyzed the style of the *Oratio pro Milone* (the final selection in the volume illustrated) to discover Cicero's mastery of the art of "moving the Passions." See below, p. 74–76, and p. 81, note 18.

The John Adams copy is a London reprint of an edition of Cicero's *Select Orations* prepared originally for use in Dutch schools. Thus, as it happens, all three of the books chosen to illustrate Adams' *Earliest Diary* had Dutch sources—an accidental but interesting indication of the international sweep of Dutch culture in the 18th century.

Courtesy of the Boston Public Library.

11. JOHN ADAMS' DIARY FRAGMENT IN THE TYLER COLLECTION, 1929

This is a detail from a larger photograph, taken (if we have read the Vermont Mutual Fire Insurance Company calendar correctly) in May 1929, when the Tyler family MSS and related materials were in the hands of the late Helen Tyler Brown, of Brattleboro, Vermont, a great-granddaughter of Royall Tyler the playwright. See the Introduction at p. 30–31. This is the only moment, so far as the present editors know, at which the MS of John Adams' earliest diary emerged to view between the 1780's, when it evidently passed from the possession of the Adams family, and April 1965, when it was identified in the Royall Tyler Collection, Gift of Helen Tyler Brown, in the Vermont Historical Society at Montpelier.

The MS appears, nearly flat, between the open volume at front left and a bound volume of *The Port Folio.* The large heading on the first page, "Harvard Colledge . . ." (as in the first illustration in the present volume), can be more or less made out.

Acknowledgments

Our first and greatest debt is to the heirs of the late Helen Tyler Brown, namely Allan D. Sutherland, M.D., and Mrs. Dorothy Sutherland Melville, and to the Director, Dr. Richard G. Wood, and Trustees of the Vermont Historical Society, for permitting us to borrow, study, reproduce, and edit for publication the precious and fragile MS of *The Earliest Diary of John Adams.*

The Honorable William R. Tyler, a descendant of Royall Tyler and currently United States Ambassador at The Hague, has taken a most helpful and continuous interest in this undertaking from a time, it may be said, before it started.

The editors of the *Legal Papers of John Adams,* Messrs. L. Kinvin Wroth and Hiller B. Zobel, have not only furnished the valuable commentary on John Adams' first legal case which is signed with their names, but have helped us solve difficult textual problems and legal questions at many other points.

We are indebted to Dr. Jules D. Prown of Yale University for the privilege of using certain findings in his two-volume study of *John Singleton Copley,* to be published in 1966 by The Belknap Press of Harvard University Press; and to Mr. David P. Wheatland of Harvard University for information on early scientific instruments at Harvard.

Mr. John E. Alden, Mrs. Elizabeth E. Butterfield, Mr. Kimball C. Elkins, Mr. Van Courtlandt Elliott, Mrs. Jane N. Garrett, Mr. Richard M. Gummere, and Dr. Clifford K. Shipton have continued their assistance to the Adams Papers in their specialties and in their invariably generous way.

The editors' sense of gratitude to the Director and staff of the Massachusetts Historical Society and to the entire organization of Harvard University Press grows keener as the Adams Papers enterprise grows older. They take especial pleasure, too, in publicly acknowledging for the first time the fidelity and competence of two relatively new members of the Adams Papers staff, Editorial Assistants Susan F. Riggs and Lynne G. Crane.

Editorial Method and Apparatus

The editorial method followed in *The Earliest Diary of John Adams* has, with slight modifications to be noted, been that followed in other parts of *The Adams Papers*. That method has been explained fully in the Introduction to the *Diary and Autobiography of John Adams*, 1:lii–lxii, and is not repeated in this small volume already overburdened with editorial matter.

In view of the nature of the material to be presented, several modifications of standing *Adams Papers* editorial policy have seemed essential or at least very desirable. First, and most important, all the entries have been printed *in the physical order in which they stand in the MS*. Although we have been successful in dating most of the entries approximately, very few beyond those that John Adams wrote and dated at Harvard can be dated exactly. Any attempt to rearrange the undated entries according to our conjectural dates would, for one thing, be impossible to carry out completely; for another, it would deprive readers of some part of the evidence on which our conjectures—or better ones—must rest. We have preferred to have readers see the jumbled Diary Fragment as nearly as possible as it was when it came from John Adams' hand. As an aid to this end, as already noted, the (editorially supplied) page numbers of the MS have been inserted throughout the text inside distinctive brackets: ⟨ ⟩.

In another respect, however, after due reflection, we have infringed on the principle just stated. We have inserted our own captions for entries that in the MS have none. These captions are enclosed in conventional square brackets and consist of appropriate titles and conjectural dates. The dates are to be considered in all cases as approximate.

Finally, in dealing with matter canceled by the diarist (always given inside angle brackets: ⟨ ⟩), we have been selective, sometimes perhaps arbitrarily so. When cancellations could not be read, they could not be transcribed and printed. And we have omitted many routine corrections. We have simply aimed to be generously representative of the diarist's first thoughts that he revised.

The guide to editorial apparatus which follows is abridged from the Guide to Editorial Apparatus which appears, with appropriate modifications, in the first volume of each of the published units of *The Adams Papers*. The reader should refer to those volumes for fuller information on devices, code names, symbols, abbreviations, &c., that are used throughout *The Adams Papers*. Only those which are used in *The Earliest Diary of John Adams* are listed in the tables below.

Editorial Method and Apparatus

TEXTUAL DEVICES

The following devices are used to clarify the presentation of the text.

[. . .], [. . . .]	One or two words missing and not conjecturable.
[. . .] ¹, [. . . .] ¹	More than two words missing and not conjecturable; subjoined footnote estimates amount of missing matter.
[ ]	Number or part of a number missing or illegible. Amount of blank space inside brackets approximates the number of missing or illegible digits.
[roman]	Conjectural reading for missing or illegible matter. A question mark is inserted before the closing bracket if the conjectural reading is seriously doubtful.
⟨italic⟩	Matter canceled in the manuscript but restored in our text.
[italic]	Editorial insertion in the text.

ADAMS FAMILY CODE NAMES

JA	John Adams (1735–1826)
AA	Abigail Smith (1744–1818), m. JA 1764
AA2	Abigail Adams (1765–1813), daughter of JA and AA, m. WSS 1786
WSS	William Stephens Smith (1755–1816), m. AA2 1786
GWA	George Washington Adams (1801–1829), grandson of JA and AA
JA2	John Adams (1803–1834), grandson of JA and AA
CFA	Charles Francis Adams (1807–1886), grandson of JA and AA

DESCRIPTIVE SYMBOLS

The following symbols are employed to describe or identify in brief form the various kinds of manuscript originals.

D	Diary
FC	file copy
LbC	letterbook copy
M	Miscellany
MS, MSS	manuscript, manuscripts
RC	recipient's copy
Tr	transcript

LOCATION SYMBOLS

The following list gives the symbols and their expanded equivalents for institutions in the United States owning original documents drawn upon in the present volume.

M-Ar	Massachusetts Archives
MB	Boston Public Library
MH	Harvard College Library
MH-Ar	Harvard University Archives
MHi	Massachusetts Historical Society

MWA   American Antiquarian Society
MiU-C   William L. Clements Library, University of Michigan
VtHi   Vermont Historical Society

OTHER ABBREVIATIONS AND CONVENTIONAL TERMS

Adams Genealogy
> A set of genealogical charts and a concise biographical register of the Adams family in the Presidential line and of closely connected families from the 17th through the 19th century. The Adams Genealogy is now being prepared for publication in preliminary form.

Adams Papers
> Manuscripts and other materials, 1639–1889, in the Adams Manuscript Trust collection given to the Massachusetts Historical Society in 1956 and enlarged by a few additions of family papers since then.

Adams Papers, Microfilms
> The corpus of the Adams Papers, 1639–1889, as published on microfilm by the Massachusetts Historical Society, 1954–1959, in 608 reels.

The Adams Papers
> The edition in letterpress, published by The Belknap Press of Harvard University Press. Since there will be no over-all volume numbering for the edition, references from one series, or unit of a series, to another will be by title, volume, and page; for example, JA, *Diary and Autobiography*, 4:205.

Min. Bk., Inf. Ct.
> Minute Books of the Massachusetts Inferior Court of Common Pleas for Suffolk County, in the custody of the Clerk of the Massachusetts Superior Court for Civil Business, Suffolk County Court House, Boston.

Q.B.
> English court of Queen's Bench.

SHORT TITLES OF WORKS FREQUENTLY CITED

AA2, *Jour. and Corr.*
> *Journal and Correspondence of Miss Adams, Daughter of John Adams, ... edited by Her Daughter* [Caroline Amelia (Smith) de Windt], New York and London, 1841–1842; 2 vols.

Adams Family Correspondence
> Adams Family Correspondence, ed. L. H. Butterfield and others, Cambridge, 1963– .

BM, *Catalogue*
> *The British Museum Catalogue of Printed Books, 1881–1900*, Ann Arbor, 1946; 58 vols. *Supplement, 1900–1905*, Ann Arbor, 1950; 10 vols.

Col. Soc. Mass., *Pubns.*
> Colonial Society of Massachusetts, *Publications*.

DAB
> Allen Johnson and Dumas Malone, eds., *Dictionary of American Biography*, New York, 1928–1936; 20 vols. plus index and supplements.

DNB
Leslie Stephen and Sidney Lee, eds., *The Dictionary of National Biography*, New York and London, 1885–1900; 63 vols. plus supplements.

Eng. Rep.
The English Reports; 176 vols. A collection and translation into English of all the early English reporters.

Ford, ed., *Statesman and Friend*
Worthington C. Ford, ed., *Statesman and Friend: Correspondence of John Adams with Benjamin Waterhouse, 1784–1822*, Boston, 1927.

JA, *Corr. in the Boston Patriot*
Correspondence of the Late President Adams. Originally Published in the Boston Patriot. In a Series of Letters, Boston, 1809[–1810]; 10 parts.

JA, *Diary and Autobiography*
Diary and Autobiography of John Adams, ed. L. H. Butterfield and others, Cambridge, 1961; 4 vols.

JA, *Legal Papers*
Legal Papers of John Adams, ed. L. Kinvin Wroth and Hiller B. Zobel, Cambridge, 1965; 3 vols.

JA-AA, *Familiar Letters*
Familiar Letters of John Adams and His Wife Abigail Adams, during the Revolution. With a Memoir of Mrs. Adams, ed. Charles Francis Adams, New York, 1876.

Jefferson, *Papers*, ed. Boyd
The Papers of Thomas Jefferson, ed. Julian P. Boyd and others, Princeton, 1950– .

Laws of Mass. (1807).
Laws of the Commonwealth of Massachusetts, Boston, 1807; 3 vols.

Mass.
Massachusetts Reports, Exeter and Boston, 1804– .

Mass., *House Jour.*
Journals of the House of Representatives of Massachusetts [1715–], Boston, reprinted by the Massachusetts Historical Society, 1919– .

Mass., *Province Laws*
The Acts and Resolves, Public and Private, of the Province of the Massachusetts Bay, Boston, 1869–1922; 21 vols.

Mass. Soldiers and Sailors
Massachusetts Soldiers and Sailors of the Revolutionary War, Boston, 1896–1908; 17 vols.

MHS, *Colls., Procs.*
Massachusetts Historical Society, *Collections* and *Proceedings*.

Morison, *Three Centuries of Harvard*
Samuel Eliot Morison, *Three Centuries of Harvard, 1636–1936*, Cambridge, 1936.

Nieuw Ned. Biog. Woordenboek
P. C. Molhuysen and others, eds., *Nieuw Nederlandsche Biografisch Woordenboek*, Leyden, 1911–1937; 10 vols.

Odell, *Annals N.Y. Stage*
George C. D. Odell, *Annals of the New York Stage*, New York, 1927–1949; 15 vols.

OED
> *The Oxford English Dictionary*, Oxford, 1933; 12 vols. and supplement.

Pick.
> Octavius Pickering, *Pickering's Reports* (Massachusetts Reports, 1822–1839), Boston, 1853–1864; 24 vols.

Quincy, *Figures of the Past*
> Josiah Quincy [1802–1882], *Figures of the Past, from the Leaves of Old Journals*, ed. M. A. DeWolfe Howe, Boston, 1926.

Salk.
> William Salkeld, *Reports of Cases in the Court of King's Bench, . . . from the 1st of William and Mary to the 10th of Anne*, London, 1721–1724; 3 parts.

Shipman, *Common Law Pleading*
> Benjamin J. Shipman, *Hand-book of Common-Law Pleading*, 3d edn. by H. W. Ballantine, St. Paul, 1923.

Sibley-Shipton, *Harvard Graduates*
> John Langdon Sibley and Clifford K. Shipton, *Biographical Sketches of Graduates of Harvard University, in Cambridge, Massachusetts*, Cambridge and Boston, 1873–   .

U.S.
> *United States Reports, Supreme Court*, Boston, N.Y., and Washington, 1875–   .

Webster, 2d edn.
> *Webster's New International Dictionary of the English Language, Second Edition, Unabridged*, Springfield, Mass., 1957.

The Earliest Diary of John Adams

June 1753–April 1754
September 1758–January 1759

Introduction

1. THE EARLIEST DIARY OF JOHN ADAMS

In shaping the necessarily complex plan of a comprehensive edition of the papers of the Adams family, the editors decided to prepare and publish first the Diary of John Adams, with its important though fragmentary supplement, his Autobiography written long after he had given up keeping a diary.[1] Among many good reasons for this decision, one was strictly practical and especially persuasive. The editors supposed they could assume, if they could assume anything, that the entire MS of John Adams' Diary, as it survived at the time of Adams' death in 1826, had been jealously kept in the hands of the family, had been passed on without loss from one generation of custodians of the Adams family archives to another, and had been transferred intact to the Massachusetts Historical Society as a gift of the Adams Manuscript Trust in 1956, two years after the Adams editorial enterprise had begun operations at the Society.[2]

Nothing has yet invalidated these assumptions. In view of the numerous and conspicuous gaps in Adams' Diary, the possibility had of course occurred to the editors that portions of this remarkable personal record might have been accidentally or even deliberately destroyed *before* 1826. In advising his grandsons to keep diaries John Adams himself confessed that he had "burned Bushells of my Silly notes, in fitts of Impatience and humiliation, which I would now give anything to recover."[3] But the "Silly notes" were letters (of which many, especially early letters, are known from other evidence to be missing from John Adams' papers), whereas, so far as the editors know at present, Adams nowhere speaks of losing or destroying any part of his Diary. Furthermore, the many short runs of entries and even whole months and years missing from the "paper booklets" of the original Diary are much more plausibly accounted for by Adams'

[1] *Diary and Autobiography of John Adams*, ed. L. H. Butterfield, Leonard C. Faber, and Wendell D. Garrett, 4 vols., Cambridge, Mass., 1961; reissued in paperback, 4 vols., N.Y., 1964.
[2] For a description of the MS of the Diary, running to some fifty parts, and an account of the transmission of the family papers, see the Introduction to JA, *Diary and Autobiography*, 1:xli–xliv, xxiii–xxxvii.
[3] JA to GWA and JA2, 3 May 1815 (Adams Papers).

I

admitted habit of writing diary entries only when he felt like doing so than by supposing he lost or destroyed portions of a record he obviously valued. The possibility, therefore, that any fragment of the Diary might have strayed during Adams' lifetime and survived to this day, unknown, outside the family archives seemed to the editors so remote as to be negligible.

And yet, not quite four years after publication of what the editors believed was an edition of John Adams' Diary complete so far as the original survived, they learned that precisely such an implausible incident had occurred at least once without leaving a perceptible trace in the family's voluminous records to suggest that it had happened.

If this can be called an editorial oversight, it is now being rectified as promptly as possible. In the present volume is printed a fragment of John Adams' Diary that begins in June 1753, more than two years earlier than the first entry (dated 18 November 1755) in the Belknap Press edition published in 1961. Although the evidence concerning its leaving the hands of the family is wholly circumstantial, it must have done so in the early 1780's, when Adams was in Europe, and he seems not to have missed it when he returned home in 1788, or afterward. It was discovered and identified in April 1965 as John Adams' earliest diary by Wendell D. Garrett, associate editor of *The Adams Papers*, in the Royall Tyler Collection (Gift of Helen Tyler Brown) at the Vermont Historical Society in Montpelier. Upon identification it was promptly and generously made available to the editors of *The Adams Papers* by the heirs of the late Helen Tyler Brown and the director and trustees of the Vermont Historical Society, and was brought to the Massachusetts Historical Society for study and editing.

For the weekend of July Fourth the Harvard University News Office released a news story on the discovery of "John Adams' Lost Diary." The interest it evoked, measured by the column inches devoted to it in the newspapers of nearly every state from Maine to California, not to mention papers in London and Rotterdam, surprised everyone concerned. But perhaps no one should have been surprised, considering the combination of appeals the story had: a 200-year-old mystery unraveled, a romantic episode in the life of young John Adams, his daughter's broken engagement, and the unfailingly entertaining style in which John Adams, from youth onward —and perhaps even earlier if earlier documents from his hand could be found—wrote about himself and the world around him. The treatment of the release on the copy desks around the nation furnished a diverting index to popular taste. There were sober leads that could be informative, like "John Adams' Harvard Days Recalled in Diary Found in Montpelier" (Boston *Sunday Herald*), or uninformative, like "Diary Throws New Light on John Adams" (Sioux Falls, So. Dak., *Argus-Leader*), "Old Adams Diary Found Revealing" (Dallas *Times Herald*), or "Manuscript of Patriot's Diary Found" (Roanoke, Va., *World News*). But with two 18th-century romances to play with, few copy editors could be so restrained. In California typical leads were: "John Adams' Love Life Revealed in New Diary" (Redding *Record-Searchlight*) and "John Adams, of Colonial Fame, Also a Lover" (Stockton *Record*). But elsewhere, too, "Teen-Ager" (or "Teener") Adams "Pined for" or was "Beguiled" or "Enthralled" or "Entranced" by "the Fair Orlinda," and his affair with this "Damsel," "Girl Friend" (sometimes "Girlfriend"), or "Mystery Miss" was "Bared by" the newly discovered manuscript, which in one instance had just emerged from "the Mist of Time." Hardly subtler were the headlines that asked in various ways "Who Was the Fair Orlinda?" or lured readers on with such a quoted tidbit as "That Face, Those Eyes!" Perhaps two short and contrasting leads covering the same news story can best conclude this excursion into headlinese. According to the Pawtucket-Central Falls, R.I., *Times*, "The Love Bug Bit John Adams," while the neighboring Taunton, Mass., *Gazette* delicately intimated: "John Adams' Mind Not Always on Law."

The extent of the news coverage reinforced the Adams editors' earlier decision, warmly supported by Harvard University Press, to publish the new MS immediately, even though this will require two editions of it that will presumably not be identical. The main purpose of the present separate edition is to place in the hands of those who have the four-volume Belknap Press edition of 1961 or its paperback reprint of 1964 [4] as good a text and as good annotation as can now be furnished, in a volume that can be shelved with those volumes. But both text and annotation must be considered as preliminary. When the first part (the *Papers of John Adams*) of Series III (*General Correspondence and Other Papers of the Adams Statesmen*) of *The Adams Papers* is issued, the first volume will include, probably as the first item, the definitive text of what we here designate as the Diary Fragment, together with annotation revised appropriately for that setting. This will mean, on the one hand, substantial reduction of the present commentary and, on the other hand, correction of both

---

[4] Issued by Atheneum Publishers.

text and notes in the light of further information and discoveries. (For example, we may still hope that more of John Adams' earliest correspondence, now so meagerly represented in the Adams Papers files, will come to light.) Since the "new" MS served Adams not only as a diary but as letterbook and general memorandum book, the editors believe it will fit in with his earliest correspondence and other writings quite as well as with his *Diary*.

2. THE MANUSCRIPT DESCRIBED AND DATED

The MS of the Diary Fragment found in April 1965 consists of twenty-eight closely written, unnumbered folio pages of paper bearing a watermark of the style known as "Arms of England."[5] The sheets were originally stitched together in a somewhat unusual pattern (to be discussed below) and have no protective cover. Except for the large size of the pages (approximately 12¼ by 7⅜ inches), the gathering thus resembles the homemade "Paper Books" in which John Adams wrote his Diary for many years.[6] Toward the back of the gathering certain pages were badly browned from exposure over a long period of time to bad atmospheric conditions, and, when found, the MS had tears and mutilations from wear at the inner hinges and outer edges and corners. Some of the corners and some fragments of the edges were ready to drop off, and a few had disappeared for good. One leaf was torn through its lower half so badly as to leave a great fragment of text precariously dangling and to make handling of the MS for close study and transcription next to impossible.

During the summer of 1965 this damage was checked from further progress by the work of an expert paper conservator, Mr. John Washeba of Medford, Massachusetts. Mr. Washeba cleaned and humidified the MS as a whole and joined the tears and filled in the mutilated areas of each sheet with chemically inert paper fibers. It can now be handled for close study.

And it has required close study, for it is a complex document in every respect. Problems concerning its physical make-up and history, its handwriting, the order and dates of entries, and its relation to John

---

[5] Its design is the quartered arms of England within a circle surrounded by the motto HONI SOIT [QUI] MAL Y PENSE, surmounted by a crown and with a bell depending below. It is a slight variant of W. A. Churchill, *Watermarks in Paper ...*, Amsterdam, 1935, No. 213. Occasional specimens of paper with this watermark have been found elsewhere among JA's papers that are known or conjectured to date from the 1750's. An example is his second Diary booklet (D/JA/2), kept in 1758–1759.

[6] See Introduction to JA, *Diary and Autobiography*, 1:xli–xlii.

Adams' other surviving records have been numerous and challenging. Most of them have now been satisfactorily solved; a few remain baffling.

As to the problem of its physical make-up, which bears materially on the original order and probable dates of the entries:

John Adams started with eight full-size sheets of paper about 14¾ by 12¼ inches in size, folded them once, stitched them loosely together with two separate loops of linen thread passed through the fold near the top and the bottom of the gathering, and thus produced a booklet of sixteen leaves or thirty-two pages of the size already stated. He numbered none of them, made his entries at irregular intervals over a long period of time (as the changes in handwriting style, as well as the substance, suggest), entered some of them backward from the other end of the booklet from that with which he began, entered others both right side up and upside down in blank pages and spaces he had left the first time through, and slit out some entire leaves at times and for purposes unknown.

To tell the story of the composition of this earliest Diary it is necessary to supply numbers for the pages of the MS. The editors have done so, and though they offer the following analysis with apologies for its technicality, it is essential to telling that story. For those who wish to follow the details, these editorially supplied page numbers have been inserted in the text itself, inside distinctive brackets or braces: ⁌{   }⁍. (They are also used around those page numbers in the following commentary and in the notes throughout the volume.)

The center fold of Adams' original thirty-two-page booklet came, of course, between pages 16 and 17. But the leaf which would have made pages 15 and 16 was slit out, leaving only a stub, and three later leaves in succession, which would have been pages 21 through 26 of the gathering, also remain only as narrow stubs. It is the present editors' opinion that in cutting out these leaves Adams wanted to write something else rather than to suppress something he had already written.[7] At any rate, having reduced his booklet by eight pages, he

[7] Their reasons are: (1) No trace of writing can be detected on the stubs, though JA tended to write close to the margins throughout most of the MS. (2) At the point where the single leaf was removed, the substance of the passage runs continuously across the gap in the MS; this gap falls *within* JA's draft letter to Tristram Dalton; see below, p. 66, and p. 68, note 5. (3) At the point where the three stubs occur successively, there appears to be no gap in the text, although here one cannot pronounce with certainty because the break is between separate paragraphs of reflection on the nature of genius and on the diarist's own deficiencies; see below, p. 73, and p. 81, note 17.

There is at least the possibility that the leaves cut out were used for one or

thereafter had one of only twenty-four. Toward the end of it, however, he embarked on a subject that profoundly concerned him—the case of Field *v.* Lambert, the first legal action in which a client engaged him as counsel. Memoranda and queries relating to this case spilled over into the first of his pocket diaries (begun in November 1755, kept spasmodically in 1756, and resumed in October 1758); but, to accommodate more notes on it, he now added, as we must suppose, another full sheet to the folio gathering we have called the Diary Fragment. This was not wrapped around the gathering but placed at the end as a separate fold perhaps loosely caught by a new pair of threads to the main gathering.[8] The added sheet of two leaves constitutes pages ⊰{ 25–28 }⊱ of the MS as it stands today.

The first page ⊰{ 25 }⊱ of this supplement is badly discolored, and the first leaf ⊰{ 25–26 }⊱ is the one, alluded to above, that was torn through a great part of its text. Now, if the final, loosely attached or unattached sheet had been folded over the real front of the booklet, or had been inadvertently placed there, several things could easily have happened that seem to have happened. Page ⊰{ 25 }⊱ would then have been the uppermost page of the booklet and would be especially subject to the effects of poor storage conditions and careless handling. The present ⊰{ 24 }⊱ (the last page of the main gathering) would have been the exposed final page of the MS and therefore subject to similar effects; it is, in fact, badly faded. At this point another physical characteristic observable in the MS becomes of interest—its three lateral creases. If for some indefinitely long period the MS was stored flat and suffered the deterioration at front and back just described, clearly for another long period it was folded and then folded again laterally to make a thickish packet one quarter of its original full page size and in the shape often given to documents in 19th-century offices for docketing and storage.[9] At the point where the first fold was made—in the middle of the page—the text of ⊰{ 24 }⊱ has faded beyond legibility from wear,

more of the fair copies of the letters drafted in the Diary Fragment. However, although the recipient's copy of the letter to Cranch (draft at p. 69, below) has the watermark found in the Diary Fragment, it does not, from its shape, appear to have been cut from that MS, and the recipients' copies of the other letters drafted in the Fragment have not been found.

[8] Since the additional folded sheet of four pages long ago silently parted from the rest of the MS and is so badly worn

at the hinge as to reveal no thread holes, its mode of attachment, if any, is conjectural. It may in fact never have been physically attached to the original gathering. Another explanation may be that the gathering as a whole was not stitched until after JA needed and added these pages.

[9] What the sequence of these two events was in the physical history of the MS cannot be determined and scarcely matters.

it being on one of the outer creases; [10] and one of the two areas exposed by the second folding was the top quarter of ⊰{ 24 }⊱, which is one of the very few spaces in the entire MS that Adams himself did not fill up with writing. In this blank space, where a docketing notation would normally go, someone wrote in an early 19th-century hand:

> Apparently—
> A Diary kept by R Tyler in 53 to 58.

To this someone else, parenthetically but very sensibly, later added:

> (As R. Tyler was born in 1757 the
> above conjecture is mistaken)

Here, however, investigation of who wrote the Diary Fragment and how it came to repose in Royall Tyler's papers seems to have ended until 1965. The MS begins with a bold and clear heading, "Harvard Colledge June 8th. 1753," which, since the early entries are obviously those of an undergraduate, limits the possible authors to relatively few persons. What is more, several of the letters drafted in the MS bear headings showing that they were addressed to members of the Harvard class of 1755, and one of the drafts is actually signed "J.A.," the initials of John Adams, A.B., Harvard 1755. This telling clue, however, was not followed up, and John Adams' earliest Diary continued to repose unrecognized among the papers of Royall Tyler in Vermont.

Admittedly the substance as well as the physical form and condition of the MS is at first sight confusing and scarcely attractive. Speaking strictly, the document is not, except for its first few pages, a diary at all, but a disorderly miscellany or catchall—part diary, part student notes on lectures, part letterbook, part commonplace-book entries, part notes on legal reading and cases, all jumbled together in what at first look like several hands, and running from both ends of an overworked and fragile MS. Such a potpourri as this in the hand of any other young man, even from the 1750's, would have limited interest. But since this is in all probability the earliest personal record kept by John Adams, and since he could not put quill to paper without revealing himself in an engaging way, the effort of deciphering so curious a document and unraveling its puzzles has had its rewards.

The MS starts with five pages of entries, brief in themselves and largely devoted to the weather, kept by Adams as a junior sophister at Harvard. These run, with breaks and a collective entry for the

---

[10] This passage is in one of JA's drafts of a writ in the case of Field *v.* Lambert, p. 94, below.

summer, fall, and early winter, from 8 June 1753 through 19 March 1754. The diarist then left three pages blank before beginning his notes on a series of lectures by Professor John Winthrop on "experimental Phylosophy," which ran from 1 through 11 April 1754 and fill five more pages. Clearly his intention was to fill up the pages left blank with retrospective entries for the rest of March. (He left ample space because he had begun to grow rather discursive in his entry of 19 March.) But his intention failed, and much later, displaying a habit of filling up blank pages and blank portions of pages that was to become characteristic, Adams used the tempting space for a comparison of the moral sense among men and animals, notes on a few pages of Van Muyden's abridgment of Justinian, and "Criteria" for determining the "Excellence of a Language."

These entries inserted later near the beginning of the Diary Fragment are, like nearly everything else in the MS except the entries made at Harvard, undated. When were they written? It is possible to answer this question with some precision and in fact to define the span of time—actually two fairly short spans of time separated by four years—during which all the entries in the Fragment were written. But to do so will require further tedious details.

The entries made at Harvard pose no chronological problems. They begin more than two years earlier than any other known diary entries made by John Adams, and all of them are either precisely or approximately dated in 1753 and 1754. The variations in handwriting throughout the MS, particularly among the early entries, which are at first so disconcerting as to suggest that this miscellany must have been composed by more than one writer, are scarcely troublesome after comparisons are made with other surviving documentation in Adams' hand. Throughout life Adams varied between a cramped and minuscule hand that he ordinarily used when writing for himself alone (as in his Diary and in taking notes on his reading or in a courtroom) and a large, bold, round, and well-spaced hand that he used for other purposes, especially in formal and official letters and papers. Both the large and small hands are found in the Diary Fragment, the large hand, however, somewhat surprisingly being employed for the entries in 1753, which constitute essentially a journal of the weather. (Did he anticipate the possibility that Professor Winthrop might look over this meteorological record?) There is a further complication. Beginning with the collective entry for 29 June 1753–January 1754 (entirely written in 1754) and persisting through the rather full notes on Winthrop's scientific lectures ending 11 April 1754, the entries are in a style of handwriting that, if seen by itself, would be hard to recognize as John Adams'. It is a relatively large hand, but much more angular than Adams' usual large hand, the slant of the words to the right is more pronounced, the formation of certain letters (notably the lower-case "d's," which have much fuller loops, even whorls, finishing the ascending stroke) is different, and the appearance of initial capital letters is much less frequent than in Adams' familiar early hand.[11] The variant hand would be a real puzzle if examples of it could not be found in other early papers written by Adams. These are regrettably meager, none at all being known for 1753–1754, with one exception to be mentioned below. But without going into detail the general statement may be made that parallel experiments with the variant hand we have been describing are to be found in Adams' letters of 1755 and early 1756 and that his Diary entries for the same period show definite traces of this hand. They vanish from his papers altogether in the course of 1756.[12] We may say further, then, that during his college years, like many other undergraduates before and since, John Adams experimented with his handwriting and that he continued to do so, with diminishing interest, for a year or so afterward. By late 1756, when he became twenty-one, his handwriting had fully matured and become stable. The one rewarding consequence of his experimentation is that his editors are now able to assign to Adams and to date with confidence certain entries in his early and interesting Literary Commonplace Book that were questionably his and that could not be dated at all.[13] It is now clear that the Commonplace Book, though mainly dating from 1756, was begun as an undergraduate, probably in 1754 since the handwriting of the first pages exactly matches the notes on Winthrop's lectures in that year found in the Diary Fragment.

On 16 July 1755 John Adams commenced bachelor of arts, and, as he recalled, at "the publick Exercises ... was somewhat remarked as a Respondent" by the Reverend Thaddeus Maccarty of Worcester, who had been "empowered by the Select Men of that Town to procure

[11] For the variant hands in the Diary Fragment see the pages reproduced in facsimile as illustrations in the present volume.

[12] See, for the progression of the variant hand from its most pronounced form back toward JA's normal hand, his letters to Nathan Webb, 1 Sept. 1755 (Adams Papers); to Jacob Bailey, Jan. 1756 (original not found; facsimile in William S. Bartlet, *The Frontier Missionary: A Memoir of the Life of the Rev. Jacob Bailey, A.M.*, Boston, 1853, between p. 34–35); to Charles Cushing, 1 April 1756 (original not found; facsimile in *The Month at Goodspeed's*, 19:134 [Feb. 1948]); and to Richard Cranch, 29 Aug. 1756 (Adams Papers).

[13] M/JA/8 in the Adams Papers; Microfilms, Reel No. 187.

them a Latin Master for their Grammar School." Maccarty engaged Adams. Early in August he rode from Braintree to Worcester and entered on his duties.[14] He did not find schoolteaching inspiring, but his *Diary* for 1756 furnishes some entertaining pictures of a schoolmaster's life in a New England village and, supplemented by his few surviving letters and his Commonplace Book, some account of his intellectual activity. Unfortunately, all of these break off by or before the autumn of 1756. On 22 August of that year Adams recorded that he had "compleated a Contract with Mr. [James] Putnam, to study Law under his Inspection for two years," and on the 23d that he "Came to Mr. Putnams and began Law. And studied not very closely this Week." [15] There are no further entries until early October 1758, the point at which Adams returned to the family home in Braintree and began his struggle to build a practice in the law.[16] The lack of documentation for the important years of Adams' legal apprenticeship has always been frustrating to his biographers and editors, and one of the first thoughts that crossed the editors' minds when the Diary Fragment came to light was that it might very well help to fill this distressing gap. Unhappily it does not. The chronological gap between the Harvard entries and the next matter in the Fragment is more than four years. In other words Adams took up this booklet again at the very same time that he resumed writing his regular Diary, in October 1758.

The conclusion just stated anticipates the evidence on which it is based. Since the post-1754 matter in the Fragment is scarcely dated at all and does not always appear in the chronological order in which the particular entries were written, further analysis is necessary.

Immediately following the undergraduate entries are drafts of three letters, undated but with their recipients identified by the writer as (John) Wentworth, one of Adams' Harvard classmates; (Tristram) Dalton, another classmate; and Samuel Quincy, a member of the Harvard class of 1754 with whom Adams had been on friendly terms. The first sentence of the first letter announces that Adams' letters will henceforth come "not from a School House [in Worcester] but from the Cell of an Hermit" in Braintree, where "Old Roman Lawyers and dutch Commentators" are his "constant Companions." Both the other letters also deal with Adams' commitment to pursue the law. It seems

[14] JA, *Diary and Autobiography*, 3: 263.

[15] Same, 1:42, 44.

[16] Nor is the gap satisfactorily filled in by letters. There are only four on record from JA for the two years Sept. 1756–Sept. 1758, three of these dating in Sept.–Oct. 1756 and the fourth in April 1758.

likely that, coming in close succession as they do, all three letters belong to the earliest days or, at most, weeks following Adams' return home from Worcester. This move he recorded in the first entry of a fresh booklet in his regular Diary, under date of 5 October 1758, as having taken place the day before, adding: "I am this Day about beginning Justinians Institutions with Arnold Vinnius's Notes. I took it out of the Library at Colledge." [17] Here a Roman lawyer and a Dutch commentator are combined in a single book, surely the book, or one of the books, playfully alluded to in the letter to Wentworth.

So it would appear that at this point, having resumed his practice of keeping diary entries in pocket booklets, Adams decided to convert his folio paper booklet into a letterbook. (Hitherto he had kept only loose copies or drafts of such of his outgoing letters as he kept at all.) Meanwhile he proceeded quite faithfully with his regular Diary entries through October, furnishing precious biographical information that is of incidental value in dating materials in the newly discovered MS. But in November he fell off again, composing only four entries, and less than a dozen in December. This meagerness is at least partly explained by the perfectly whimsical way in which he recurred during these months to the folio booklet for miscellaneous jottings when it was within easier reach. There is no real distinction in substance or form between what went into his "regular" Diary at this period and what went into his older, larger miscellany, except that he gave slightly more attention to dates (usually, however, only the day of the week) in the pocket booklets which he had come to think of as his real Diary.

The material in the folio MS following the three letter drafts is miscellaneous indeed. It embodies classical quotations applied to some of Adams' contemporaries, disapproving comments on his own temperament and working habits, and an essay on human genius of different sorts (Adams wonders if he just possibly has genius of *any* sort) which gradually becomes a discussion of how Cicero as an orator and Milton as a poet accomplished their aim of "moving the Passions." Parallel passages abound in Adams' regular Diary during the final three months of 1758, but others of the same kind may be found in 1759 and even later, so that they help little in arriving at precise dates for the new material. Embedded in this series of miscellaneous entries are two letter drafts. The second of these is essentially a literary exercise and offers no clues to its date. The first, which deals with a young lady

[17] First entry in "Paper Book No. 2" as numbered by CFA, the family archivist and editor; D/JA/2 in the Adams Papers arrangement. Text is in JA, *Diary and Autobiography*, 1:44; see also p. 45, notes 1–3.

fancifully named Orlinda, is more interesting and of some help. Although the recipient is not named in the MS, the undated and unsigned recipient's copy, with a slightly variant text, addressed to Adams' close friend and (later) relative by marriage, Richard Cranch, long ago found its way back to the Adams Papers and is preserved there.[18] Of the fascinating and, for a long time, rather mysterious "O." or "Orlinda," and young John Adams' relationship with her, we now know a good deal. She was Hannah (1736–1826), daughter of Colonel Josiah Quincy of Braintree. A tireless flirt, she captivated Richard Cranch and Anthony Wibird, and at one point very nearly ensnared John Adams and herself in a net of her own weaving. The story of their affair can be followed in scattered entries in Adams' *Diary* as published in 1961. The first reference to her occurs in an undated entry probably written early in January 1759, where the diarist records a grave conversation between himself and "H.Q. or O." (he later crossed out "H.Q. or" and left only "O.") over a tea table at her father's house. The subject was the conduct of husband and wife toward each other—always an agreeable topic for young people in love. "O. thinks more than most of her Sex," Adams commented in his Diary. "She is always thinking or Reading"—good things to do if one's target is a studious young lawyer.[19] Soon after this he felt obliged to record that she affected more candor and familiarity than she really felt: "Her face and Hart have no Correspondence." [20] But he was still seeing her frequently and reported with regrettably few details a sentimental stroll he took with her one evening from what is now Quincy Square (where her father's house was) to the Vassall-Borland house (now the Adams National Historic Site), through the Borland farm, and home by way of present Presidents Hill.[21] Here are the oscillations of feeling usual in such cases. In the spring came a very narrow escape for Adams, when only the accidental interruption of an ardent conversation with Hannah by two of their young friends saved him from a commitment to marriage against which he had been warned and for which he was far from ready.[22] On her side, Hannah was saved for Dr. Bela Lincoln of Hingham, whom she soon married. On his side, Adams thought the episode "a great sacrifice to Reason," and for a time he keenly regretted it. In his first encounters with Abigail Smith at the Weymouth parsonage, for example, he found her seriously wanting in "fondness" and "Tenderness" when compared with Hannah

[18] Adams Papers, Microfilms, Reel No. 343, under the assigned and erroneous date 1761–1765.

[19] *Diary and Autobiography*, 1:66–67; see also p. 71, note 2.

[20] Same, p. 68.

[21] Same, p. 72; see also p. 74, note 1.

[22] Same, p. 87.

Quincy.[23] But before long he knew he had done best and had no further regrets.

The draft letter to Cranch about Orlinda in the Diary Fragment must have been written after Adams' return to Braintree early in October 1758. (Up to that point, and even a little beyond it if we take note of allusions in a letter to his friend Crawford further on in the Diary Fragment, Adams had been interested only in Worcester girls.) How soon afterward is a matter of conjecture. The language is so extravagant as to suggest that the writer is not entirely serious, but behind the extravagance is some measure of feeling—the earliest expressed by John Adams for Hannah Quincy. At a guess, the letter dates from November or December 1758, just before Adams' interest in Josiah Quincy's attractive daughter became decidedly serious.

The letter about Orlinda is followed by a sequence of notes mostly devoted to a legal case with which John Adams was concerned during the same final three months of 1758. The case was that of Field *v.* Lambert, first tried in Josiah Quincy's court (for Hannah's father was a justice of the peace as well as a colonel of militia) between two of Adams' neighbors. Two of Luke Lambert's horses had broken through a fence and trampled some of Joseph Field's crops. At the very moment Field was trying to turn them out and drive them to the town pound, Lambert appeared and "rescued" them out of Field's hands without offering to pay for the damage they had done. Field brought suit, but there were technicalities, set forth in great detail in Adams' regular Diary entries of 13 October and 5? November 1758.[24] Up to this point Adams seems to have been simply an interested observer of the proceedings; now Field retained him to bring a new action. It was the fledgling lawyer's first case and greatly excited and worried him. Queries, memoranda, notes, and draft documents concerning it appear indiscriminately in both his regular Diary and the Diary Fragment. On 18 December, according to the regular Diary, Adams "delivered to Mr. Field a Declaration in Trespass for a Rescue," partial drafts of which appear in the Diary Fragment.[25] He felt that despite his heroic efforts the paper was "quite indigested and unclerklike," feared that it would prove defective, and then people would say that "I dont understand my Business." It did prove defective, as he reported on 29 December. "Fields Wrath waxed hot," and Adams suffered agonies of humiliation.[26]

[23] Same, p. 108–109.
[24] Same, p. 48–50, 57–58.
[25] Below, p. 93–96.
[26] *Diary and Autobiography*, 1:62–63, 64–65. In the Editorial Note referred to in the following footnote the question is raised whether the *Diary* entry assigned to the date of 29 Dec. 1758

So complex are the questions both of law and chronology in Field *v.* Lambert that a commentary on it in the form of a special Editorial Note, prepared by L. Kinvin Wroth and Hiller B. Zobel, the editors of the *Legal Papers of John Adams,* has been inserted ahead of the relevant entries in the text of the Diary Fragment.[27]

Since all the entries relating to this case in both of Adams' personal records clearly belong to the final months of 1758, it now begins to appear more and more as if everything in the newly discovered MS, beyond the Harvard entries dated in 1753–1754, must belong to those months too unless definite evidence can be found to the contrary.

No such evidence is forthcoming, although the closing date, for reasons that will appear, should probably be kept a little flexible. Sandwiched among the notes on Field *v.* Lambert in the Fragment is the draft of an undated letter to William Crawford, a Princeton graduate who preached in and around Worcester during the years Adams taught school and trained for the law there. This letter tells "how I live" in terms similar to those in Adams' letters to his Harvard friends, described above, and was no doubt written at about the same time, but the note of nostalgia for Worcester friends, particularly a girl in Worcester named Betsy Greene, suggests a relatively early date within the three-month span. Following the entries relating to the Field case is another undated draft letter addressed to Crawford that can probably be more definitely dated. This engaging letter tells of a recent visit the writer had made to Boston and does so in a style consciously reminiscent of John Gay's celebrated *Trivia: or, The Art of Walking the Streets of London.* Adams' published *Diary* records three visits to Boston in October and one in November 1758.[28] Although there may have been still others, not recorded, there is good reason to believe that the letter to Crawford describes Adams' visit of several days near the end of October. The Suffolk Inferior Court was in session, and he had interviews with Jeremy Gridley and other leading lawyers to arrange for his admission to the bar, attended court, and went to an evening party with Samuel Quincy, where he encountered (as he wrote in a fine Pepysian phrase) "the finest Row of Ladies, that ever I saw." [29] These incidents appear to be reflected in his letter to Crawford, and it must therefore have been written in the last week of October or early in November.

---

may not actually have been written a week later.

[27] See Editorial Note on the Case of Field *v.* Lambert, p. 82–89, below.

[28] *Diary and Autobiography,* 1:47, 51, 54–57, 58–59.

[29] Same, p. 54.

In the physical sequence of items in the new Fragment this leaves three "last" entries to be taken into account. Their diversity illustrates the formlessness of this miscellany. First is a little run of very carelessly written student notes on civil law; second, some observations on Shakespeare's characters and figurative language, illustrated with quotations; and third, some rather cryptic notes supporting a petition (text not present) from certain Braintree men who had enlisted for a campaign against Canada but had failed to receive the bounty payments they thought themselves entitled to. The passage on Shakespeare, as one might expect, offers no clues as to when it was written and is thus of no help in dating the adjacent jottings. The notes on the Braintree petition, which appear upside down on the very last page of the folio gathering, relate to a matter that terminated in the Massachusetts House of Representatives on 10 January 1759, when the petition was read and dismissed.[30] Thus the notes were written prior to that date, probably when Adams was advising his neighbors, the petitioners, on the preparation of their appeal. How much earlier can only be guessed at, but certainly after he had set up his law office in Braintree in October 1758 and, at a guess, in the month before the petition came up in the General Court.

To return now to the first of the last three entries in the Diary Fragment: Baffling at first since they seem to start with a hopelessly unsyntactical sentence ("Judicial are ..."), these notes turn out to be a continuation without break in substance of student notes entered much earlier in the MS. Specifically they continue the notes on a lawbook identified by the editors (Adams never cites the author, title, or page references) as Johannes van Muyden's abridgment of Justinian's *Institutes*, inserted at a very early point in the MS, among those pages left blank in the undergraduate entries of 1754. It is possible to say almost exactly when the notes were written. On 26 October 1758, during his visit to Boston to talk with the leaders of the bar, Adams recorded in his regular Diary that "Mr. Gridley lent me Van Muydens Compendiosa Institutionum Justiniani Tractatio in usum Collegiorum. Editio tertia prioribus Auctior et emendatior." [31] Adams was looking at this volume as he wrote this entry; after Gridley's death he purchased it; it survives in the Adams collection in the Boston Public Library, and its titlepage is reproduced as an illustration in the present volume. The young lawyer did not advance rapidly in his reading of Van Muyden. On 20 December he recorded that he was resuming the

---

[30] See the editorial discussion of this passage at p. 104, note 4, below.
[31] *Diary and Autobiography*, 1:56.

Tractatio "at the 99th Page." [32] Assuming (although with young John Adams this is not a safe assumption) that he was reading the book in sequence, the notes on Van Muyden in the Diary Fragment, drawn from pages 114–124, were put down in late December 1758 or early in January 1759. No other notes by Adams on Van Muyden or references to reading his book have been found except a retrospective one in June 1759. [33]

Emerging from this long detail of the evidence bearing on the date or dates when John Adams wrote his earliest Diary, the fragmentary and very miscellaneous document before us, we can conclude with assurance that he made use of it at two different periods: in 1753 and 1754, as he himself indicates, while he was at Harvard, to record weather memoranda, small incidents of college and personal life, and notes on certain lectures that interested him; and then again, and apparently exclusively, more than four years later, during the first three or, at most, four months, October 1758–January 1759, following his return to his father's house in Braintree to undertake the practice of law. In the second of these periods he used it for all sorts of purposes that have been described above, and a very untidy and often cryptic thing he made of it. This conclusion still leaves wholly unfilled the two-year gap of September 1756–September 1758. In the opinion of the editors, it is far more likely that one or more diary booklets or catchall collections of reading notes and miscellaneous memoranda once existed for those two years and are now lost than that any of the entries in the present MS, even those entirely without clues to their dates, help to fill the gap. The discovery of *The Earliest Diary of John Adams* in the papers of a figure only peripherally connected with the Adams family raises all sorts of questions in the midst of what seemed certainty. Are there still other, perhaps even earlier, fragments of his Diary, other records of his reading in literature and the law, other fragile and unidentified gatherings of retained copies of his letters, early or late, still extant? Who will find *them*?

3. THE HISTORY OF THE MANUSCRIPT RECONSTRUCTED

How did this earliest personal record composed by John Adams escape from his own and his family's hands and turn up, more than two hundred years after it was written, among the papers of Royall Tyler in Montpelier, Vermont?

The answer seems clear, but, like everything else connected with

[32] Same, p. 63. [33] Same, p. 103.

this document, it is not simple and cannot be furnished without some elaboration of details. The story involves the Adams family's transatlantic wanderings, a romance that looked promising but ended unhappily, and a certain amount of plain carelessness and forgetfulness on the part of a number of people.

At some point sooner or later after filling up his folio gathering with diary entries, letter-drafts, and miscellaneous memoranda, Adams put it away with his other papers and may never have looked at it again. Certainly he seems not to have missed it, for up to the point of going to press the present editors have found no explicit mention of it among his formidable mass of papers. However, the editors have not read everything Adams ever wrote, and the Diary Fragment could possibly have been among the records relating to his Harvard years to which he did allude as totally lost in a letter written many years later to David Sewall, then his only surviving classmate:

> I had preserved all my calculations of eclipses, my theses and blundering latin syllogisms, . . . in a chest by themselves; but when I became a wanderer from home, they all disappeared, and whether they were employed by my clerks to light their pipes or my girls to cover their pies, I know not, but I have not a scrap of a single college paper left in the world.[34]

There is no mention of a college diary here, and from the fact that the Diary Fragment contains as much matter related to Adams' early law studies and practice as to Harvard, it seems far more likely that the MS was filed with his legal papers than with his old college exercises when Adams began his decade of diplomatic service. His departure from Braintree for Europe in February 1778 was sudden and secret;[35] he was home again only for a brief and extremely busy period in 1779;[36] everything concerning his farm, his legal business, and his books and papers had to be left to his wife. Adams had great confidence in her ability to handle all such things well. And so, everything considered, she did. But in the matter of the Diary Fragment she may have committed a *gaffe*.

The year 1782 John Adams spent largely in the Netherlands, where, as the fruit of two years of tireless labor on his part, greatly aided by the defeat of Cornwallis' army in Virginia, he won recognition from the States General of the independence of the United States. In October, having negotiated a loan of five million guilders by a syndicate of Dutch bankers to the Continental Congress and having signed a treaty

[34] 4 Nov. 1821 (LbC, Adams Papers).
[35] See JA, *Diary and Autobiography*, 2:269–270; 4:1–7; *Adams Family Correspondence*, 2:370–389.
[36] See JA, *Diary and Autobiography*, 2:400–402.

of amity and commerce between the two powers, he hastened to Paris to join Benjamin Franklin and John Jay in negotiating provisional articles of peace between Great Britain and the United States. Despite these accomplishments and certain clear signs that the war was drawing to a close, Adams was feeling more lonesome and put-upon than ever. The year before, he had permitted his eldest son and constant companion on these diplomatic tours of duty, John Quincy, to go with Francis Dana to St. Petersburg, and he had sent Charles, his second son, home because Europe did not seem to suit either his temperament or his health. And so, though he was intensely occupied with affairs of the highest concern to his country, Adams thought often and longingly about his family and farm near Boston.

At home were Mrs. Adams, daughter Abigail, and the two younger boys, Charles and Thomas Boylston. Young Abigail being seventeen, her father might have expected at almost any time the sort of news that his wife sent him in a letter dated 23 December 1782:

[W]e have in the little circle an other Gentleman who has opend an office in Town, for about nine months past, and boarded in Mr. Cranch['s] family. His Father you knew—his name is Tyler. He studied Law upon his comeing out of colledge with Mr. [Francis] Dana, but when Mr. Dana went to congress he finished his Studies with Mr. Angier.[37] Loosing his Father young and having a very pretty patrimony left him, possessing a sprightly fancy, a warm imagination and an agreable person, he was rather negligent in persueing his buisness in the way of his profession; and dissipated two or 3 years of his Life and too much of his fortune for to reflect upon with pleasure; all of which he now laments but cannot recall. . . . His mamma is in possession of a large Estate and he is a very favorite child. When he proposed comeing to settle here he met with but little encouragement, but he was determined upon the trial, he has succeeded beyond expectation, he has popular talents, and his behaviour has been unexceptionable since his residence in Town; in consequence of which his Buisness daily increases. He cannot fail making a distinguished figure in his profession if he steadily persues it. I am not acquainted with any young Gentleman whose attainments in literature are equal to his, who judges with greater accuracy or discovers a more delicate and refined taste.[38]

[37] Oakes Angier, of West Bridgewater, who had been a law clerk to JA; see *Adams Family Correspondence*, 1:83–84; JA, *Legal Papers*, 1:lxxxi. AA seems, however, to have been mistaken. No one else mentions Angier as Tyler's law preceptor after the latter left Dana's office. Dana himself said that Tyler continued his clerkship with Benjamin Hichborn, a young Boston lawyer (Dana to JA, 23 May 1783, Adams Papers). This is confirmed by an entry in the Suffolk Bar Book (MS, MHi); see MHS, *Procs.*, 1st ser., 19 (1881–1882):154. On Hichborn see JA, *Diary and Autobiography*, 2:174–175; 3:318–319.

[38] Adams Papers. In publishing this letter in the several editions of his grandmother's correspondence which he edited, CFA silently omitted from the text

18

Such detailed and approving comment could be a prelude to only one thing, and Mrs. Adams, who was obviously captivated by Tyler's urbane manners and literary graces (and knew she was), put it as skillfully as she knew how to her absent husband:

I have frequently looked upon him with the Idea that you would have taken much pleasure in such a pupil—I wish I was as well assured that you would be equally pleased with him in an other character, for such I apprehend are his distant hopes.

She could see "a growing attachment" on Tyler's part to Abigail, "stimulated by that very reserve" which the young lady prudently maintained in spite of her being by no means "wholy indifferent" to the attentions of such an agreeable and eligible young man. "His days are devoted to his office, his Evenings of late to my fire side," and his "distant hopes" have been expressed to Mrs. Adams in the most honorable and considerate way, in a brief but elegant letter she copied into her own for her husband to read. But what meant most to Mrs. Adams was that she observed in Tyler occasional "Sentiments, opinions and actions" that reminded her unmistakably of her husband. "Suffer me," she appealed to him in her most affectionate manner—

Suffer me to draw you from the depths of politicks to endearing family scenes. . . . I inclose you a little paper [39] which tho trifling in itself, may serve to shew you the truth of my observations. The other day the gentleman I have been speaking of, had a difficult writ to draw. He requested the favour of looking into your Book of forms,[40] which I readily granted; in the Evening when he returned me the key he put in to my hands a paper which I could not tell what to make of; untill he exclaimed "O! Madam Madam, I have now hopes that I shall one day become worthy your regard. What a picture have I caught of my own Heart, my resolutions, my designs! . . . I found this coppy of a Letter in a pamphlet with observations upon the study of the Law and many excellent remarks; you will I hope forgive the theft, when I deliver the paper to you; and you find how much benifit I shall derive from it."

It is just possible that this "endearing" scene was the very occasion on which Royall Tyler abstracted the Diary Fragment from John Adams' law office, which was a ground-floor room with its own outside door in what is today known as the John Quincy Adams Birthplace on Franklin Street in Quincy. The "paper" that he handed to Mrs. Adams

---

everything relating to Tyler and thus reduced it by more than half. See, for example, JA–AA, *Familiar Letters*, p. 410–412.

[39] Not found.

[40] JA's Pleadings Book, which survives in the Adams Papers (M/JA/7; Microfilms, Reel No. 186); it is printed with full annotation in JA's *Legal Papers*, 1:26–86.

and that at first she "could not tell what to make of" could have been the MS published in the present volume. In it are retained copies of several letters containing "observations upon the study of the Law and many excellent remarks" pertaining thereto, written by John Adams at the very outset of his career. Since the specific "coppy" Tyler made and Mrs. Adams forwarded cannot now be found, this possibility can be neither proved nor disproved. But Adams had written similar letters at other times, and if Mrs. Adams' language is precise rather than approximate, the letter that evoked Tyler's rhapsody was found "in a pamphlet," which means a printed work rather than a MS gathering. All that can be said is that Tyler had been given access to Adams' papers, that he used the privilege to see what he wished to, and that one of the uses he put it to was improving his standing with the elder Abigail. The amiable way in which she responded to this "theft" (as Tyler called it) would have made others like it easy.

A week after her first letter on this momentous subject, Mrs. Adams wrote her husband another that covered much of the same ground—a common practice because letters sometimes failed to survive Atlantic crossings and, going by different ships, often arrived out of the order in which they were written and sent. In the second letter she added more details on Tyler's personal history. After giving up the company of "the Gay and Fair . . . in a round of pleasure and amusements," he had made a trial of establishing a law practice in Falmouth (now Portland, Maine), "but his ambition and Genious could not brook a retirement like that," and so he came to Braintree and fixed both his lodgings and office at the Cranches' home, where he

has conducted with great Steadiness and application ever since. . . . If he is steady he will shine in his profession. His disposition appears exceedingly amiable—his attractions perhaps too powerful even to a young Lady possesst with as much apparent coldness and indifference as ever you saw in one character. . . . I cannot however help noticeing the very particular attention and regard of this Gentleman towards her, and that it daily becomes more pleasing to her.[41]

He is currently trying to purchase a farm in Braintree, and "if he should obtain the regard of the Lady he wishes for, I suppose he would think himself authorized to address you; but at present he is in a state of suspence." With this long recapitulation Mrs. Adams enclosed "a little poetick Scrap" (now missing) by Tyler that she thought might amuse her husband.

John Adams was not amused. He told his wife at once that, having

[41] 30 Dec. 1782 (Adams Papers).

signed the Preliminary Articles of Peace with Great Britain, he had better come home instead of considering, as he had been, her coming over to join him in Europe. As for her news about Tyler's attentions to Abigail, he said flatly:

I confess I dont like the Subject at all. My Child is too young for such Thoughts, and I dont like your Word "Dissipation" at all. I dont know what it means—it may mean every Thing. There is not Modesty and Diffidence enough in the Traits you Send me. My Child is a Model, as you represent her and as I knew her, and is not to be the Prize, I hope of any, even reformed Rake.[42]

The more he thought about it, the higher Adams' feelings mounted. A lawyer, to be sure, would be his first choice as a son-in-law, "but it must be a Lawyer who spends his Midnights as well as Evenings at his Age over his Books not at any Lady's Fire Side. . . . I am not looking out for a Poet, nor a Professor of belle Letters." Adams reminded his wife of something he supposed she very well knew, namely that, since he had given up a lucrative profession for poorly paid public service, their resources were meager. "My Children will have nothing but their Liberty and the Right to catch Fish on the Banks of Newfoundland." In one of the few known passages in which he trained his talent for sarcasm on his wife, he denounced "this Method of Courting Mothers" that he saw all too clearly Tyler was employing. In brief, he concluded, "he and you have both advanced too fast, and I should advise both to retreat."

Surprisingly, Adams' next letter was much more conciliatory. From his own knowledge and from what his wife had told him, he was aware that Tyler had wide and influential connections in Boston and had been trained under good masters, and he supposed that "if he has Health, Talents, and Application and is a Speaker, his Relations will easily introduce him to full Business." But the matter of Tyler's "Gaiety" still worried him. In Adams' judgment, "That Frivolity of Mind, which breaks out into such Errors in Youth, never gets out of the Man but shews itself in some mean Shape or other through Life." However, "I must submit my Daughters Destiny, to her own Judgment and her own Heart," supported by her mother's advice and that of other trusted counselors.[43]

The situation was a classic one, having all the elements of comedy to be found in the brilliant school of 18th-century playwrights whose work Royall Tyler so much admired and later imitated. But it had,

[42] 22 Jan. 1783 (Adams Papers).   [43] 4 Feb. 1783 (Adams Papers).

perhaps, some potentially tragic elements too, for this drama was being enacted in real life and not on a stage.

The principal character, who had so artfully and disturbingly entered the close-knit Adams family circle, was born in Boston 18 July 1757 and was christened William Clark Tyler. His father was Royall Tyler (1724–1771), a Harvard graduate in 1743, a Boston merchant, justice of the peace, perpetual member of town committees, from 1764 a member of the Governor's Council, and according to the Hutchinsonian party a great meddler and self-seeker in the affairs of Harvard College and the Province.[44] This was because, although he belonged by birth and occupation to the Province's mercantile establishment, the elder Tyler took the popular side on most questions and cultivated the good will and support of the Boston "mechanicks." Encountering John Adams as a rising young lawyer in 1770, Tyler "began to pick chat" with him, recommended to him a curious mixture of reading (which Adams took quite seriously) that included "Dr. Souths sermon upon the Wisdom of this World," Mandeville's *Fable of the Bees*, Halifax's *Character of a Trimmer*, "Hurds Dialogue upon Sincerity in the Commerce of Life—and Machiavell and Cæsar Borgia." [45]

Although Tyler was a member of the Boston Sons of Liberty, he did not live long enough to have his political principles put to the ultimate test. Dying in 1771, he left an estate valued at £4,100 (which included "a chaise, mansion, shop, and store") and a widow, the former Mary Steel, who found solace the following year by marrying another well-to-do merchant and lived until 1800.[46] His son William Clark received a generous share of the estate and in April 1772, by consent of the General Court, took his father's Christian name Royall.[47] That same year, at the age of fifteen, he entered Harvard College and four years later commenced bachelor of arts with such a reputation for wit and literary talents that Yale conferred the same degree upon him.[48] In December of that critical year 1776 Tyler enrolled in Boston's new silk-stocking military troop called the Independent Company, of which John Hancock was colonel. But apart from marching to Rhode Island in one or perhaps in both of the unsuccessful campaigns of 1777 and 1778 to drive the British from Newport, Tyler apparently saw little action in the Revolution.[49] Sometime in 1777 he entered Francis Dana's

[44] Sibley-Shipton, *Harvard Graduates*, 11:313–318.

[45] JA, *Diary and Autobiography*, 1:362.

[46] Sibley-Shipton, *Harvard Graduates*, 11:318; Thomas Pickman Tyler, "Memoirs of the Hon. Royall Tyler, late Chief Justice of Vermont," MS, VtHi:Tyler Collection (Gift of Helen Tyler Brown).

[47] Mass., *Province Laws*, 5:181.

[48] Thomas P. Tyler, "Memoirs of Royall Tyler."

[49] *Mass. Soldiers and Sailors*, 16:240; *DAB*, under Royall Tyler. AA wrote JA

office in Cambridge to read law, but according to Dana he was there "but a short time, two or three months, if I remember right," when Dana departed to serve in the Continental Congress and "left him finally with Mr. Hitchbourn." [50] In 1780 he was admitted to practice in the Inferior Court; it is very uncertain whether he was ever admitted

from Boston, 1 Aug. 1776: "There is a fine company formed in this Town, call'd the independant Company consisting of young Gentlemen of the first families. Their Number is 80, they are the School for forming officers, they take great pains to acquire military Skill and will make a fine figure in a little while" (*Adams Family Correspondence*, 2:73).

[50] Dana to JA, 23 May 1783 (Adams Papers). See note 37, above. Dana had left Cambridge before the middle of Nov. 1777.

This was the period during which, according to Tyler's own testimony as reported in AA's letters quoted above, Tyler "dissipated two or 3 years of his Life and too much of his fortune" in the company of "the Gay and Fair . . . in a round of pleasure and amusements." There is evidence to support this testimony. At a meeting of the Harvard faculty on 20 Oct. 1777, Bachelors of Arts Samuel Sewall (Tyler's classmate, later chief justice of the Supreme Judicial Court), Rufus King (A.B. 1777, later U.S. Senator), and Tyler were reported to have drunk to excess in a tavern and caused "Great disorders," including "horrid profanity, riotous and tumultuous noises, [and] breaking of college windows." When called before the faculty, Tyler treated his questioners "with great insult and indignity," making a speech in which he declared that they had no right to punish him and that he cared nothing for "a little paltry Degree which may be bought at any time for twenty shillings." This "impropriety," or worse, was not forgotten in 1779, when Tyler became eligible for a master's degree. On 10 July of that year the faculty voted that Sewall, King, and Tyler could receive this degree only if they apologized for their behavior in 1777. Evidently they all complied, for they received their degrees. See Records of the College Faculty (1775–1781), Meetings of 20 Oct., 18 Nov. 1777; 10 July 1779 (MH-Ar).

Another purported consequence of Tyler's "dissipated" conduct during this period having been recorded by the Harvard librarian and antiquarian John Langdon Sibley, it can hardly be passed over without a mention. In his Private Journal (MS, MHi, deposited in MH-Ar), under date of 15 Oct. 1856, Sibley described an interview he had that day with a long-time resident of Cambridge who from time to time had furnished materials for Sibley's sketches of Harvard graduates. The source of these valuable recollections, Sibley says, was "Mr. Royal Morse, (illegitimate son of a woman who was a sweeper for very many years in the college buildings by a student, Royall Tyler)." A careful reading of everything that members of the Adams-Cranch circle had to say about Tyler has persuaded the present editors that no one in that circle knew of any such incident or rumor thereof, and therefore that, whether or not it was a fact, it had no influence on their opinion of him. Royal (1779–1872), son of Katherine (or Katharine) Morse (1756–1835), was a well-known and respected figure in 19th-century Cambridge, and Sibley's initials are signed to the two-column obituary of him in the *Cambridge Press*, 10 Feb. 1872, which gives his birth date as 6 June 1779. (On the Morses, see also Thomas W. Baldwin, comp., *Vital Records of Cambridge . . .*, Boston, 1914–1915, 1:501, 502; 2:668–669; Lucius R. Paige and Mary I. Gozzaldi, *History of Cambridge . . .*, Boston and Cambridge, 1877–1930, 1:231, 413, 468; 2:518; Hannah Winthrop Chapter, Daughters of the American Revolution, *An Historic Guide to Cambridge*, 2d edn., Cambridge, 1907, p. 158; Samuel F. Batchelder, *Bits of Harvard History*, Cambridge, 1924, p. 278–280.) The sole statement regarding Royal Morse's paternity known to the editors remains the parenthetical and rather casual one in Sibley's Private Journal.

to the Superior Court of Judicature or its successor, the Supreme Judicial Court.[51] After a short-lived attempt to establish a practice in the provincial town of Falmouth, seat of Cumberland County, Maine, he arrived in Braintree early in 1782, with the interesting results for the Adams family that we have seen.

The long story of Tyler's courtship of the younger Abigail Adams cannot be told here. It has recently been told in some detail elsewhere,[52] and the full documentation will be published in forthcoming volumes of *Adams Family Correspondence*. After the flurry of December 1782–January 1783, all parties moderated their mood and pace. In March, John Adams gave his wife milder instructions. "If there is a Trait of Frivolity and Dissipation left," he could only hope their daughter would "renounce" the idea of any connection whatever. "I ask not Fortune nor Favour . . . but Prudence, Talents and Labour. She may go with my Consent wherever she can find enough of these."[53] He took the precaution, however, of writing to his friend and colleague in St. Petersburg, Francis Dana, Tyler's first law teacher, for an opinion on the young man's character and his promise as a lawyer.[54] Back home, Abigail was sent to live with friends in Boston, and her mother, replying meekly to Adams' rebuke of 22 January, reported in April that she had "put a present period . . . to the Idea of a connection. To extirpate it from the Hearts and minds of either is not I apprehend in my power."[55]

The elder Adamses faced another problem that intertwined itself with the one posed by the ingratiating Tyler. John Adams had asked Congress to relieve him of his duties abroad after the Preliminary Articles were signed, and he sincerely wished to go home. But he also yearned for the appointment, sure to be made eventually, to negotiate a commercial treaty with Great Britain. Since Congress was in the throes of one of its periodic great debates on foreign affairs, the question as it presented itself to Adams, languishing in Paris while another debate in London delayed action on a definitive treaty, was: Should he go home and tend his farm and law practice, or should he wait for the appointment and instruct his family to come over and bring him some measure of the domestic comfort he missed so badly? Month after

[51] In February term, 1783, his admission to practice before the Supreme Judicial Court was taken under advisement by the Court, but no further action is recorded. Records of the Supreme Judicial Court, 1783, fol. 29 (Early Court Files, Suffolk County Court House, Boston).

[52] Lida Mayo, "Miss Adams in Love," *American Heritage*, 16:36–39, 80–89 (Feb. 1965).
[53] 28 March 1783 (Adams Papers).
[54] 24 March 1783 (MHi:Dana Papers).
[55] 7 April 1783 (Adams Papers).

month in 1783 he gave his wife contradictory advice on this subject, depending on his mood and the latest reports and rumors concerning Congress' intentions. By fall he was seriously ill from worry and frustration, and by the beginning of 1784 Mrs. Adams had decided to take the voyage as soon as weather permitted and arrangements for her absence could be made.[56] By bringing young Abigail with her she would have help in caring for Papa's health, and the total separation of the young people for a time would test the strength of their affection. (A standard device to meet a standard problem.) Tyler had recently purchased for £1,000 one of the best houses and farms in Braintree, the Vassall-Borland place, later to be so indissolubly associated with the Adams family because it was the home of successive generations of Adamses from 1788 to 1927.[57] "I should deceive you," Mrs. Adams told her husband in reporting this news, "if I did not tell you that I believe this Gentleman has but one object in view"—to advance in his profession and standing in the community "with a hope that he may not be considered unworthy a connection in this family."[58] She had already placed in Tyler's hands "Your Account Books . . . , that the whole [of the debts owed Adams by legal clients] might not be lost, by insolvent Debtors and refugee Tories as a great part already is, he is in a way to get them adjusted; some little money he has received."[59]

From Boston, Abigail wrote her mother that she would accompany her "rather . . . from necessity than choice—the latter would never carry me, the former must."[60] And at length Tyler himself wrote formally to John Adams soliciting "the Sanction of your Approbation to my Addresses" and to a union between Abigail and himself upon her return[61]—then not expected to be more than a year later. Although the reply he had received to his inquiry of Dana about Tyler had not been all that he had hoped for, Adams took Tyler's request with composure—now that his daughter was coming to Europe for a cooling-off period. His cordial answer said that he approved of Tyler's family, his education and profession, and his purchase of a home and farm in Braintree. Furthermore, "The Testimonials I have received of your personal Character and Conduct are such as ought to remove all Scruples upon that head." Abigail is to make her own choice in due time, but she is now coming to Europe. If in the meantime "my Library may be of Use to you, in the Prosecution of your Studies or your Prac-

---

[56] JA to AA, 7 Sept. 1783; AA to JA, 3 Jan. 1784 (both in Adams Papers).
[57] See above, p. 12, and references in note 21 there.
[58] 27 Dec. 1783 (Adams Papers).
[59] 3 Jan. 1784 (Adams Papers).
[60] 6 Jan. 1784 (AA2, *Jour. and Corr.,* 2:28–29).
[61] 13 Jan. 1784 (Adams Papers).

tice, the loan of it is at your Service." [62] Accordingly, just before sailing for England in June, Mrs. Adams instructed her uncle, Dr. Cotton Tufts, left in charge of all the Adamses' affairs in Braintree, that "The Library [is] to be under the care of Mr. Cranch. No Books to be lent out unless to him and Mr. Tyler without your permission. . . . Mr. Adams account Books to be left in the hands of Mr. Tyler who is desired to collect what Debts are due, and pay the same to you." [63]

Thus Tyler was left in possession of Lawyer Adams' account books and with a free run of his large library. Presumably Adams' papers were with his books, although we have no way of telling what measures Mrs. Adams took for safeguarding her husband's extensive files of private, business, and official papers. In their account of Adams' office methods and records, the editors of the *Legal Papers of John Adams* concluded (before the Diary Fragment was found) that segments of his financial records as a lawyer are missing from his papers at the Massachusetts Historical Society. [64] But it is extremely unlikely that Adams would not have missed such records, if they had indeed disappeared while he was absent abroad, and that he would not have attempted to recover them after coming home in 1788. And we have Cotton Tufts' express word that Tyler eventually, though tardily, returned all documents of this sort to Tufts in the summer of 1786. [65] It would have been easy, however, for Tyler to have overlooked an isolated piece like the Diary Fragment, whether borrowed before or after the Adams ladies' departure for Europe.

The Adamses were thrillingly reunited in London in August 1784. [66] During the following ten months they occupied an imposing but cheerful villa at Auteuil, on the outskirts of Paris, where Adams served, with Franklin and Jefferson, as a commissioner to negotiate commercial treaties between the United States and numerous European and North African powers. In May 1785, Adams having been appointed first minister plenipotentiary from the United States to the Court of St. James's, the family made their way to London and began hunting for a suitable legation. Affairs between young Abigail and her suitor in America had apparently failed to go well from the time their separation began. According to her mother, Abigail was constantly busy at her writing desk, and it is known that by October 1784 Tyler had received her portrait in miniature. [67] But Tyler wrote little and irreg-

[62] 3 April 1784 (FC in JA's hand, Adams Papers).

[63] 18 June 1784 (MiU-C).

[64] JA, *Legal Papers*, 1:lxxiii and notes there.

[65] Tufts to AA, 15 Aug. 1786 (Adams Papers), quoted below, p. 28.

[66] See JA's and AA2's accounts of the reunion in JA, *Diary and Autobiography*, 3:170–171.

[67] See Mary (Smith) Cranch to AA, 10 Oct. 1784 (Adams Papers).

ularly, and he was under the heavy disadvantage of lodging in the house of his fiancée's aunt, a woman who let nothing he did pass unobserved or uncommented on. Mrs. Cranch's comments were not all unfavorable, especially at first, but before long she reported that Tyler was "but little at home," liked to drive about in a sleigh, sulked when he did not receive frequent letters, and boasted when he received many —without responding in kind.[68] In Auteuil, Abigail pined in silent dejection, the meaning of which was only too clear to her mother. After two or three months in London without hearing from Tyler, the young lady came to a decision. In a letter which consisted of only a single sentence but covered a packet containing Tyler's miniature and the few letters he had written her, she requested him to turn over her miniature and letters to her Uncle Richard Cranch and tartly expressed the hope "that you are [as] well satisfied with the affair as is A.A." [69] Mrs. Adams wrote a long letter of explanation to Mrs. Cranch. During the year she had been in Europe young Abigail had received but four letters in all from Tyler and only a single short one in the seven months of 1785. His insistence that he has written more, all the Adamses are convinced, is prevarication and shows a want of "strict honour" on his part that compels the breaking off of the engagement. Abigail "appears much more cheerfull since she has unburdened her mind." As for the effect on Tyler, Mrs. Adams doesn't suppose "it will kill him. . . . I have always told him, that he was his own greatest enemy. Such he has proved. I do not wish," she concluded, "that a syllable more may be said upon the subject." [70]

She was not to have her wish. A great deal more was bound to be spoken and written on the broken romance. Mrs. Cranch reported that Tyler for a time continued to act as if nothing had happened, though at one point he announced he would go to London and "settle every misunderstanding"—which he attributed entirely to Mrs. Cranch's gossiping—and steadily refused to give up Abigail's letters.[71] Eventually he had to, for word came from London sometime before the summer of 1786 that Abigail was engaged to Colonel William Stephens Smith of New York, late of the Continental Army and currently secretary of

[68] To AA, 25 April 1785 (Adams Papers).

[69] Undated but undoubtedly written in Aug. 1785. This is the only letter from AA2 to Tyler known today, and its text cannot be vouched for because the original has not been found. The text here quoted is in Elizabeth (Hunt) Palmer's recollections as printed in *Grandmother Tyler's Book: The Recollections of Mary Palmer Tyler (Mrs. Royall Tyler), 1775–1866*, ed. Frederick Tupper and Helen Tyler Brown, N.Y. and London, 1925, p. 76.

[70] 15 Aug. 1785 (MWA).

[71] To AA, 10 Dec. 1785, 9 Feb. 1786 (both in Adams Papers).

legation in London. Smith had pushed his suit with soldierly vigor, and the couple were married in June.[72] "Some of her Friends wish it had not been so Sudden," Mrs. Cranch commented, and the family records contain intimations that Mrs. Adams wished so too.[73]

Tyler had been full of bustle and ventures in Braintree during the spring, but the ventures did not prosper. At the Borland place he erected a windmill which was to power a chocolate mill and a bolting mill. "I wonder," Mrs. Cranch remarked, "if the Law business is to go by wind also." [74] Dr. Tufts could never find him when he wanted to settle the Adams accounts; Tyler failed to attend meeting even when he was in Braintree; and it was soon apparent that he was having difficulty financing his Braintree property and paying the workmen who had repaired and erected buildings there.[75] Ultimately the property reverted to the Borlands. Tyler had lost interest in it, as he had in everything else in Braintree. The last we hear of him there is in August 1786, when he "voluntarily" handed over to Dr. Tufts John Adams' "Acct. Books, Notes of Hand and some other Papers, his Acct. for Business done I expect to have in a few Days." [76] He had long since given up his lodgings at the Cranches and was living in Boston. Family tradition records that he was so stunned by the news of Abigail's marriage that he "closed his office and spent the succeeding summer in the retirement of his mother's house at Jamaica Plains." [77]

The winter of 1786–1787 was the time of the Shaysite disturbances in the western counties of Massachusetts. Major General Benjamin Lincoln took command of the state forces in January and appointed Tyler an aide-de-camp with the rank of major.[78] To judge from his letters that have been preserved and the reports of his hard riding from one post to another in western Massachusetts, in Vermont (where he had his first view of the state he later settled in), and in New York, the aide relished his work. Early in March he was sent on a mission to

---

[72] See the article by Lida Mayo cited above in note 52; also Katharine Metcalf Roof, *Colonel William Smith and Lady: The Romance of Washington's Aide and Young Abigail Adams*, Boston, 1929.

[73] Mrs. Cranch to AA, 2–3 July 1786 (Adams Papers). In a letter of 21 March (MWA), AA had asked her sister: "[W]hat shall I do with my young Soldier, who is much too zealous to be married, and will hardly give me time to tell my Friends that such an event is like to take place. I have no Idea of such a hurry, and so I tell him."

[74] To AA, 22 March 1786 (Adams Papers).

[75] Cotton Tufts to AA, 13 April 1786; Mrs. Cranch to AA, 2–3 July, 28 Sept. 1786 (all in Adams Papers).

[76] Tufts to AA, 15 Aug. 1786 (Adams Papers).

[77] Thomas P. Tyler, "Memoirs of Royall Tyler." See also *Grandmother Tyler's Book*, p. 76.

[78] Thomas P. Tyler, "Memoirs of Royall Tyler."

New York City to discuss means of apprehending Shaysite fugitives in that state. New York obviously gave Tyler's social and literary proclivities more scope than Boston, to say nothing of Braintree. The actor-manager Thomas Wignell was looking for a native American play that would suit his own talents as a comedian, and Tyler, who may never have been inside a theater before, obliged by writing *The Contrast* in a few weeks. A comedy of manners imitative of Sheridan but broader in its humor and more farcical in its action, *The Contrast* was produced at the John Street Theatre on 16 April 1787, and thus Tyler became "the first playwright of American origin to have his work brought out by professional actors." [79] The play is perhaps more memorable for presenting the first stage Yankee, Jonathan, who boasts that the deacon's daughter he is about to marry will bring him as dowry "Twenty acres of rock, a bible, and a cow," and who is as full of "tarnals" and "nations" as Yankee Doodle. Wignell played this part to great acceptance, and the embryonic school of New York theater critics characterized the play as undoubtedly a work of genius. But its interest here lies in the fact that, while Tyler's knowledge of the dissolute world of fashion that he chiefly satirized must have derived from reading books imported from London, his observation of Yankee character, manners, and language had been most recently in the Adams-Cranch circle at Braintree. "The "Contrast" that gave him his title is between, on the one hand, Dimple, an Anglicized New York gallant and avowed disciple of Chesterfield who fatally ensnares himself in his amorous and mercenary intrigues, and, on the other hand, Colonel Manly, a rustic New Englander who supposes that a coat is something to keep oneself warm in, is quick and effective in rescuing virtue from distress, and speaks gravely (and tediously) about the merits of Christian morality, plain dealing, and patriotism. Where Royall Tyler thought he himself may have fitted in the scale between these two extremes, is a question one cannot help asking, but there is no way to answer it. When word reached Mrs. Adams in London of the success of *The Contrast*, she assumed that "The comedy writer has been drawing his own Character and an other Gentlemans" (i.e. William Stephens Smith's).[80] In this she seems to have been quite mistaken. It is doubtful if Tyler took either of his character types very seriously; his purpose was to entertain, and he accomplished it. The smart from his loss of Abigail Adams, however sharp, seems to have dissipated in the course of his military service and his exposure to the heady air of New York.

[79] Odell, *Annals N.Y. Stage*, 1:255. (owned by J. Delafield DuBois, New
[80] AA to Mrs. Cranch, 16 July 1787 York, N.Y., 1957).

Braintree people heard promptly about the theatrical venture, and they made the expected comments. Play-acting being still under a ban in Boston, Mrs. Cranch was not likely to be edified by the thought of "a Man writing comedys in one state while he is suffering his interest in another to be all taken by execution and sold at Vendue, even to the Boards and lumber which he had got to repair his House and *Mill* with." She advised her sister and brother-in-law Adams to buy the house for occupancy on their return from Europe.[81] As soon as they could send instructions to Dr. Tufts, this was done.

Although the next few years were exceedingly restless ones for Royall Tyler, he had a versatile, productive, and distinguished career ahead of him, mainly in Vermont, where he went to live in 1791, as a man of letters, lawyer, judge, professor of law, and paterfamilias.[82] In 1794 he married Mary Palmer (1775–1866), whom he had first encountered in Braintree as a little girl and later in the household of her father, Joseph Pearse Palmer, where Tyler had lodged in Boston.[83] Mrs. Royall Tyler outlived her husband by forty years and left reminiscences that furnish, among other things, an account of Tyler's courtship of young Abigail Adams that is interesting but in some respects as fanciful as the plot of *The Contrast*.[84] The Tylers' life together was long and happy, much longer and happier than that of the William Stephens Smiths.

Tyler died at Brattleboro, Vermont, in 1826, where he had lived since 1801 and where descendants of his still live. His papers were left to his family, each generation of which furnished at least one member who took a constructive interest in Judge Tyler's career and writings. Forty years ago the late Helen Tyler Brown (1864–1935), a great-granddaughter, prepared with the aid of the late Professor Frederick Tupper an edition of her great-grandmother's recollections and

[81] To AA, 22 April–20 May 1787 (Adams Papers).

[82] The most authoritative sketch of Tyler is still that by Arthur Hobson Quinn in *DAB*, but it is disappointingly brief.

[83] Through the Cranches the Palmers were connected with the Adams family. AA's sister, Mary (Smith) Cranch, was married to Richard Cranch, whose sister was Mary (Cranch) Palmer, wife of Brig. Gen. Joseph Palmer, father of Joseph Pearse Palmer and grandfather of Mary (Palmer) Tyler. See Adams Genealogy under all these names. The Joseph Palmers lived at Friendship Hall in the Germantown section of Braintree; there are many references to them and some correspondence with them in the Adams Papers. See indexes to JA, *Diary and Autobiography*, and *Adams Family Correspondence*.

[84] *Grandmother Tyler's Book*, p. 76–80. Mrs. Tyler explained the seemingly erratic conduct of Tyler toward AA2 and the animosity of the Cranches toward Tyler on the ground of his addresses to the Cranch girls—addresses that were deliberately *pretended* because Tyler wanted to prove the Cranch ladies' jealousy of their cousin and niece AA2.

issued it, with related materials and appropriate illustrations and family trees, as *Grandmother Tyler's Book*, which has been several times cited in this Introduction. It was Miss Brown's fervent hope and expectation that a book-length biography of Royall Tyler would one day be written and published by those whose interest had been aroused by "Grandmother's" book. She had spent much of her life gathering materials to fill out the story left partially told by her great-uncle, the Reverend Thomas Pickman Tyler, in his "Memoirs" of Royall Tyler, the MS of which she possessed, and she traveled and corresponded widely in pursuance of her aim. But the difficulties were great, and the task proved too much for her. In 1932, when representatives of the Vermont Historical Society showed keen interest in acquiring the papers and promoting her project, she added a codicil to her will by which she left all the materials she had inherited and collected to three trustees, "to be used in preparing, compiling and publishing a biography of the said Royall Tyler," whereafter they were all to be given outright to the Vermont Historical Society.[85] The papers were thereupon placed in the Society's library, but by her direction were kept as a "closed exhibit," accessible only to the trustees she had named. Miss Brown died in 1935, and in the end her plan (and the terms of her will) failed through the death of all the trustees before the biography was written. Since scholarly interest in early American literature and history rose spectacularly during the 1940's and 1950's, there was naturally much curiosity about what Tyler's papers might contain, but it could not be gratified. At length in 1963, at the instigation of the Society and members of the Tyler family, the two heirs of Helen Tyler Brown on the one hand and the Vermont Historical Society on the other came to an agreement that promised a solution to the problem. By this legal instrument all of the papers (with the exception of some that were to be retained as microfilm copies) were deeded to the Society, to be kept together and designated as the Royall Tyler Collection, Gift of Helen Tyler Brown. They were to be made immediately available for research by qualified persons, permission by one or the other of the two heirs being requisite during the first five years after the agreement, but access thereafter to be unrestricted. Approval of this "equitable and workable program to carry out, so far as possible at this time, the wishes of the late Helen Tyler Brown" was given by Judge Beatrice J. Brown of the Marlboro District Probate Court on 1 May 1964.[86]

[85] Agreement between the heirs of Helen Tyler Brown and the Vermont Historical Society, 1963–1964, Vt. Hist. Soc., *News and Notes*, 15:84 (July 1964).

[86] The full text is in the Society's

Among those most curious about the contents of the Tyler Collection, from the time they first learned of its existence, were the editors of the Adams Papers. They knew that, all told, a good many letters had passed between Royall Tyler and members of the Adams family during an intensely interesting period of several years beginning in 1782. Some of these letters the editors had on record in one form or another, and others were known from allusions in the family correspondence, but the gaps were conspicuous.[87] Somewhere a packet of love letters—if not originals, then copies—might exist, and it was important to find out whether Tyler's papers would furnish any of these or clues to them, for use in the *Adams Family Correspondence*, the first two volumes of which, ending in 1778, were published in 1963 and further volumes of which are in active preparation. In brief, Mr. Garrett went to Montpelier in the spring of 1965 hoping to find love letters. He found none, and only a single original Adams letter of any kind, that written by Mrs. Adams to Tyler on 14 June 1783, containing a sufficiency of sober advice, from herself and her husband, on how Tyler should conduct himself during his state of probation. But in an unmarked manila folder among the miscellaneous items in this very miscellaneous collection Mr. Garrett did find the MS of what we take to be, although it would be folly to be too positive about it, John Adams' *earliest* Diary.

4. YOUNG JOHN ADAMS

Cluttered and fragmentary though it is, the new Diary illuminates young John Adams' mind and personality in a surprising number of ways. It does more, for it deals with some matters that were of concern to its author throughout his life and thus gives us intimations of Adams the lawyer, statesman, thinker, and man.

We had always supposed that Adams did not begin keeping a diary until after his graduation from Harvard and that it took the earthquake of 1755 to jolt him into doing so.[88] The new Diary starts with the beginning of Adams' third year at college and covers, with gaps, most of the academic year 1753–1754. Up to now we have had no contemporaneous evidence at all on his life as an undergraduate and

---

News and Notes (as cited in the preceding note), p. 84–86.

[87] One gap can be easily accounted for and is not likely to be filled. The letters AA2 recovered from Tyler were presumably destroyed by her. If not, they were lost in the fire that in 1862 con-

sumed AA2's other papers in the home of her son-in-law at Fishkill Landing (now Beacon, N.Y.); see *Adams Family Correspondence*, 1:xxx.

[88] JA, *Diary and Autobiography*, 1: xiii, 1.

little enough about it in the form of recollections by himself or others. His account in his Autobiography of his admission to Harvard under the kindly eye of Tutor Mayhew is charming and famous.[89] In the letters he exchanged with his classmate David Sewall in 1821–1822 there are allusions to an "Epitaph" (said to have been written by Adams) on certain "Greasey Tables" burned in the college commons; to Adams' noisy imitation of George Whitefield's revivalistic preaching; to "our play-reading Club"; and to the classmates' going "up on the roof of Old Harvard [Hall], to view, with a Tellescope, the Sattelites of Jupiter, and gaze at the ring of Saturn." [90] A few other scraps of this kind may be found in Adams' late correspondence, but all told they do not add up to much, and Adams himself recorded in 1821 that a chest containing all his college themes and calculations had long since disappeared.[91]

The early entries in the Diary Fragment thus throw a strong beam of light where there was none before, and, read carefully, provide clues to how Adams began what was to become one of the most valuable personal records of the 18th century. The very first entries (8–29 June 1753) are essentially a weather record. New Englanders had always kept records of the weather, commonly in almanacs on blank pages that were inserted for the purpose. This was because most of them were farmers and much concerned with the prospects of their crops. It is easy enough to say that John Adams, a Braintree farmer's son, was simply following a practice of his elders, and of course he was. But this does not explain why he began to do so when he did. His first entry ("At Colledge. A Clowdy, Dull morning . . .") was put down on the first day of a new college quarter or term. The following twenty-one entries, put down without a break until the end of recitations preceding the senior examination, commencement, and the long summer vacation, all either deal exclusively with or at least take account of the weather. But at an early point among them, small events—such as who preached and from what texts, the theses disputed by the class, reading and lectures, and a ride to Watertown—begin to intrude. The weather record was thus becoming a true diary, but the regularity of the weather observations and their exact congruence with the period the writer attended classes suggest a real, if undefined, relationship between Adams' diary-keeping and his studies. This is reinforced by the

[89] Same, 3:259–260.
[90] Sewall to JA, 14 Dec. 1821 (Adams Papers); JA to Sewall, 26 Nov. 1821 (RC owned by Pierce Gaines, Fairfield, Conn., 1964; LbC in an amanuensis' hand, Adams Papers).
[91] See above, p. 17 and note 34.

fact that the entries cease altogether upon his return home at the end of June.

The most significant addition to the curriculum for junior sophisters at Harvard was instruction in natural philosophy, with laboratory demonstrations, by the Hollis Professor of Mathematics and Natural Philosophy, John Winthrop, who was much the most distinguished member of the Harvard faculty during John Adams' years in college.[92] Among Winthrop's wide scientific interests none was more central than his meteorological and climatological studies. The value he attached to the daily observation and recording of the weather is plain from his own Meteorological Journal, kept with the utmost fidelity from 1742 until within a few days of his death in 1779.[93] In the 1750's it consisted of readings twice daily of the barometer, of Hawksbee's and Fahrenheit's thermometers, of wind direction and velocity, and general weather observations quite similar in length and character with those made by his student John Adams.

We cannot say that Winthrop's injunction or example caused young John Adams to begin a diary of the weather that became a diary for many other purposes, because we do not know this for a fact. But it seems likely. Certainly Winthrop's influence was pervasive throughout the academic year that Adams recorded in the Diary Fragment. The longest entry that Adams composed in 1753, that of 20 June, is devoted to a lecture by Winthrop on "the sphæroidall form of the earth" and to scientific reading in Nieuwentijdt's treatise apparently done in connection with it.[94] And the entries beginning 1 April 1754, comprising the second half of Adams' undergraduate journal, are entirely devoted to the notes taken on each of the eight lectures delivered that term in Winthrop's "series of Experimental Phylosophy." [95] When Winthrop's lectures stopped, so did the Diary.

How deeply did Winthrop's influence penetrate? Did young John Adams come close to choosing a scientific career? The answer to the first question would seem to be: Quite deeply. And to the second: Not very close. In his Autobiography Adams testified that "Mathematicks and natural Phylosophy attracted the most of my Attention" while in college, and although he supposed that a better knowledge of the classics might have been more useful to him in the career he did choose, "I owe to this [scientific training] . . . perhaps some degree of Patience of Investigation, which I might not otherwise have obtained." [96] The

[92] On Winthrop see below, p. 46, note 2.

[93] MS, 3 vols., owned by the American Academy of Arts and Sciences, deposited in MH-Ar.

[94] Below, p. 45–46.

[95] See below, p. 60–64, and p. 61, note 2.

[96] *Diary and Autobiography,* 3:262; see also p. 260.

habits he formed while under Winthrop's tutelage of recording meteorological data, of making observations on natural phenomena, for example on earthquakes,[97] and of pondering the system of the world, long persisted in his pocket diaries and to a lesser extent in his correspondence; and in his old age his interest in cosmology revived and grew stronger than ever. All his life Adams had a roving, absorbent mind that responded to stimuli from any quarter of the intellectual world. Association with amateurs of science in Philadelphia during his service in the Continental Congress led him to tell his wife, almost at the moment that he signed the Declaration of Independence, that "If ever I get through this Scene of Politicks and War, I will spend the Remainder of my days, in endeavouring to instruct my Countrymen [he meant New Englanders] in the Art of making the most of their Abilities and Virtues. . . . A philosophical society shall be established in Boston." [98] Association with French scientists in Paris reinforced his determination. Among the noteworthy accomplishments of his life was one he set on foot during the few months in 1779 he spent at home between diplomatic missions. This was his plan, which had to be left to others to carry out, for founding the American Academy of Arts and Sciences. Significantly, Adams made this proposal at a dinner in honor of the Chevalier de La Luzerne, the new French minister to the United States, tendered by the Harvard Corporation and held in "the Philosophy Chamber" of Harvard Hall, that is, in the late Professor Winthrop's lecture and apparatus room.[99] The Academy was chartered in 1780. Adams served as its president for many years and as a generous patron even longer.

But both external circumstances and his own temperament prevented John Adams from becoming a scientist. The circumstances, which were the political events of the time, are too well known to need explanation. Even with a different conjunction of them, however, there is no strong likelihood that he would have been drawn to science professionally. Nowhere does Adams intimate that he felt himself endowed with that "Genius" which he recognized in the great scientific innovators. Lacking that, he seems to have felt even as early as 1758, in the Diary Fragment itself, that work in science became too readily the grubbing up of facts and data, the collecting and contemplation of "Cockell shells and Pebblestones," pleasurable but no more than a

---

[97] See his marginalia in Winthrop's *Lecture on Earthquakes* . . ., Boston, 1755, which are printed in *Diary and Autobiography*, 1:61–62, 201–202.

[98] 3–4 Aug. 1776 (*Adams Family Correspondence*, 2:75).

[99] JA to Benjamin Waterhouse, 7 Aug. 1805 (MHi:Adams-Waterhouse Coll., printed in Ford, ed., *Statesman and Friend*, p. 22–29); JA, *Corr. in the Boston Patriot*, Letter 29 (31 July 1809), esp. p. 163.

hobby. If "you had chosen the study of Nature, for the Business of your Life," he asked an unknown, perhaps imaginary correspondent, should your aim not be "to improve the Manufactures, the Husbandry, or the Commerce of Mankind," rather than "to adorn a Library with Butterflies of various sizes, Colours and shapes?" [100] A quarter of a century later Adams voiced the same impatience with scientific empiricism in a letter to his wife that has deeper implications. He was then at The Hague and had just visited a "Mr. Lionet," [101] a learned man whose "Hobby Horse has been natural Knowledge" and who had illustrated and published a folio volume about his vast collection of caterpillars.

Have you an Inclination [Adams asked] to read and inspect Cutts of the Anatomy of Caterpillars—their Names, Blood, Juices, Bones, Hair, Senses, Intellects &c. &c.—Their moral Sense, their Laws, Government, Manners and Customs.

I dont know whether he teaches the manner of destroying them, and Saving the Apple Tree.

I doubt not the Book is worth studying. All Nature is so.—But I have too much to do, to Study Men, and their mischievous Designs upon Apple Trees . . . and other Things, ever to be very intimate with Mr. Lionet, (whom I respect very much however) or his Book.[102]

Before he filled up and put away his earliest Diary in 1759 or so, John Adams had committed himself to "Saving the Apple Tree" from designing and mischievous men. Science became for him, like the fine arts, something he responded to with enthusiasm from time to time, but could take or leave alone.

As an undergraduate, however, and during the year immediately following his graduation, he faced not one but several options besides science. The usual expectation of rural families who sent their eldest sons to Harvard College in 18th-century New England was that those sons would become ministers of religion. Such was the expectation of Deacon John Adams and others among young John Adams' relatives, some of whom were clergymen.[103] In September 1754, at the beginning of his senior sophister year, Adams became a scholar on the Thomas Hollis foundation for students preparing for the ministry.[104] At the same time, as he later remembered, partly because he had been applauded as a speaker in sessions of his play-reading club, his "Inclination was . . . fixed upon the Law," although his "Judgment was not so

[100] Below, p. 71.
[101] Pierre Lyonnet (1707–1789) (*Nieuw Ned. Biog. Woordenboek,* 8: 1090–1092).
[102] 25 July 1782 (Adams Papers).
[103] JA, *Diary and Autobiography,* 3:263.
[104] MH-Ar:College Book No. 6.

easily determined." [105] When he took the post of schoolmaster in Worcester, he did so simply in order to support himself until he could make up his mind whether to "study Divinity, Law or Physick." [106]

At Worcester Adams lodged with Dr. Nahum Willard, a respectable practitioner who had a library of standard medical books. The young schoolteacher read in them and "entertained many thoughts of Becoming a Physician and a Surgeon." [107] How long or seriously he did so is anyone's guess. Quite possibly such thoughts offered him his first relief from forebodings about a ministerial career. His earliest letter that survives, addressed to a favorite cousin, was written a few weeks after he arrived in Worcester and is full of gloom: "Not a single Idea has coloured my mind this month. At Colledge gay, gorgeous prospects, danc'd before my Eyes, and Hope, sanguine Hope invigorated my Body, and exhilerated my soul. But now hope has left me, my organ's rust and my Facultys decay." On weekdays he must drudge at teaching, and Sundays are sacrificed "to the Frigid performances" of disciples of "Frigid John Calvin." [108] Years later Adams recalled that the controversy in Braintree over the Reverend Lemuel Briant's Arminian views and domestic conduct had raged during the years that he himself had been in college. "Ecclesiastical Councils were called and sat at my Fathers House," and the "Spirit of Dogmatism and Bigotry" exhibited there led young Adams to believe "that the Study of Theology and the pursuit of it as a Profession would involve me in endless Altercations and make my Life miserable, without any prospect of doing any good to my fellow Men." [109] By the time he wrote this passage Adams had seen many more and perhaps worse displays of "Dogmatism and Bigotry," and so some of his later disgust may color it. For as late as the spring of 1756 he wrote his classmate Charles Cushing that while the lawyer must rake and fumble "amidst the rubbish of . . . lignum Vitæ words" and "often foments more quarrells than he composes," and while the physician's lot is "infinite toil" without certainty of reward, the divine, whose way to be sure may be hard, has in the end the best opportunity both "to do . . . good to his fellow men and make . . . provision for his own future Happiness." [110]

This letter concluded, however, with the assurance that its writer would "not therefore very suddenly become a Preacher," and the next letter on record, written at the end of August just before the Superior

---

[105] *Diary and Autobiography*, 3:262–263.
[106] Same, p. 263.
[107] Same, p. 264.
[108] To Nathan Webb, 1 Sept. 1755 (Adams Papers).
[109] *Diary and Autobiography*, 3:262.
[110] 1 April 1756; original not found; facsimile in *The Month at Goodspeed's*, 19:134 (Feb. 1948).

Court sat in Worcester, announced to Adams' Braintree friend Richard Cranch his engagement "with Mr. Putnam to study Law with him, 2 years, and to keep the school at the same time. It will be hard work, but the more difficult and dangerous the Enterprize, a brighter Crown of Lawrell is bestowed on the Conqueror." Whatever his apprehensions may be, they are fewer than "when I thought of preaching. . . . I shall have Liberty to think for my self without molesting others or being molested my self." [111] Clearly Adams had arrived at some independent ideas on religion and was unwilling to step into an intellectual strait-jacket. To Cushing he explained his reversal since spring by saying that pious and accomplished young ministers are now despised and ridiculed if they are suspected of heterodoxy, while "sleepy stupid" ones are cried up merely because they are orthodox.[112]

For a lonely and introspective young man, a reluctant schoolteacher who missed the bustle and intellectual stimulation of Cambridge, the quarterly sessions of the Inferior Court and the annual term of the Superior Court of Judicature sitting in the shire town of Worcester in September must have offered the chief relief from the dullness of village life. A court week fell in mid-May, and although Adams did not record any cases or gossip in his *Diary*, his entry on the second day, "Rambled about all Day, gaping and gazing," is eloquent for what it implies.[113] The Sunday evening following he "spent . . . at Mr. Putnams, very sociably." [114] His *Diary* at this period contains increasingly frequent references to companionship with Putnam, hunting with him, taking tea and lodging at his hospitable house, and the like.[115] This able lawyer had long monopolized the legal business of Worcester, and it was out of Adams' association with him, of course, that the seemingly but not actually sudden decision of 21 August sprang:

Yesterday I compleated a Contract with Mr. Putnam, to study Law under his Inspection for two years. . . . Necessity drove me to this Determination, but my Inclination I think was to preach. However that would not do. But I set out with firm Resolutions I think never to commit any meanness or injustice in the Practice of Law. The Study and Practice of Law, I am sure does not dissolve the obligations of morality or of Religion. And altho the Reason of my quitting Divinity was my Opinion concerning some disputed Points, I hope I shall not give Reason of offence to any in that Profession by imprudent Warmth.[116]

Having thrown off a major source of uneasiness, Adams remained doubtful about his capacity to master the field he had chosen. "The

[111] 29 Aug. 1756 (Adams Papers).
[112] 19 Oct. 1756 (Tr, Adams Papers).
[113] *Diary and Autobiography,* 1:26.
[114] Same, p. 27.
[115] Same, p. 25–40, *passim.*
[116] Same, p. 42–43.

Law," he wrote Cranch, "I take to be a very difficult and a very extensive Science." To obtain skill in its theory and success in its practice requires "a serene head, a large Collection of Books, length of Time, and the Friendship and Patronage of the great Masters of the Profession." Did he have or could he command these requisites, and could he meet the competition of the increasingly "numerous Train" of young sons of the law now entering the profession? [117]

We cannot follow the training of this son of the law because the essential documentation is still lacking.[118] But thanks to the newly discovered Diary Fragment, we can see him with lifelike clarity at the very outset of his professional career. Here is a young man totally committed to mastering the "unlimited Field" of the law—"A Field in which Demosthenes, Cicero, and others of immortal Fame have exulted before me! A Field which incloses the whole Circle of Science and Literature, the History, Wisdom, and Virtue of all ages." Shall he, as he asks his friend Wentworth, "dare to expatiate here in full Career, like the nobler Animals, that range at large"; or shall he "blindly, basely creep, like the mole, or the weezell?"[119] The law may seem dry to the gay and the ignorant, for "Every Thing . . . is dry in Proportion as it is not understood." But for the truly inquiring mind it is the best means of "tracing to their original sources in Morality, in the Constitution of human Nature, and the Connections and Relations of human Life, the Laws which the Wisdom of perhaps fifty Centuries, has established for the Government of human Kind."[120]

This is the vein of all that follows in the next several years and in fact well beyond. Mastery of the law may be infinitely difficult, but it is the best key to self-knowledge, to understanding the springs of action in others, and to familiarity with ancient and modern history and eloquence. "Now to what higher object," Adams asked his dear friend and fellow-lawyer Jonathan Sewall in a letter written a year after his own admission to the bar—

> to what higher object, to what greater Character, can any Mortal aspire, than to be possessed of all this Knowledge, well digested, and ready at Command, to assist the feeble and Friendless, to discountenance the haughty and lawless, to procure Redress of Wrongs, the Advancement of Right, to assert and maintain Liberty and Virtue, to discourage and abolish Tyranny and Vice[?] [121]

[117] 18 Oct. 1756 (Tr, Adams Papers).
[118] See, however, the remarks of the editors in JA, *Legal Papers*, 1:liv. Their account at p. lii–xciv is by far the fullest and most authoritative yet written of JA's development as a lawyer.
[119] To John Wentworth, below, p. 65.
[120] To T. Dalton, below, p. 65–66.
[121] Oct. 1759 (Dft in *Diary and Autobiography*, 1:124).

Here are blended the intellectual, humanitarian, and civic ideals that animated Adams throughout the distinguished legal career that stretched before him.

Over and over again in a myriad ways Adams was to ask himself and others how the rewards of certainty obtainable in the exact sciences, or even the blessings from mercy to suffering fellow creatures earned by the doctor or surgeon, could be compared with the rewards of the law, which embraced every aspect of man in society:

> Why the minute Arteries and Tendons of the human Body, the organization of the human Voice, and mouth, and numberless other subjects of the like sort should be thought worthy of the Attention of a liberal Mind; and the no less Wonderful and much more important combination of Passions, Appetites, Affections, in the human Breast that operate in human society, too futile, or too disagreable, for a wise Mans Examination, I cannot imagine. . . .
>
> Nothing less than the Preservation of the Health and Properties, Lives and Tranquility, Moralls and Liberties of Millions of the human species, is the object and Design of the Law, and a Comparison of several Constitutions of Government, invented for those Purposes, an Examination of the great Causes of their Danger, as well as those of their safety, must be as Agreable an Employment as can exercise the Mind.[122]

Such was the nature of Adams' commitment, combined in this youthful passage with a prophetic chart of his contributions as a political philosopher. The problems of man in society having proved more resistant to solution than the problems of anatomy, not to mention other exact sciences, Adams was surely right in urging the priorities he did.

But in 1758 what worried the fledgling lawyer was whether he could ever rise to the ideals he so fervently believed in. He had doubts on two scores. One was external. He needed guidance, patronage, clients, money for books. The warm friendliness of the leading lawyer of Massachusetts, Jeremy Gridley, supplied him with some of these desiderata. His first client was a stingy and litigious neighbor, Joseph Field, but the case, though trifling so far as money was concerned, was technically difficult, and Adams' writ proved defective. The worst of this was that the winner was Luke Lambert, a coarse country wit and dabbler in all sorts of business—an "operator" as we would say today— who made even people who despised him laugh at his jokes and victims.[123] To be bested by Lambert in his very first case was excruciat-

---

[122] To Peter Chardon, Jan. 1761 (Dft in same, p. 196–197).
[123] *Diary and Autobiography*, 1:60, 64.

ingly humiliating for the Harvard-trained and fully accredited young lawyer who proposed to introduce professional standards of practice in Braintree. Trying to find excuses, he complained that it was his "Destiny to dig Treasures with my own fingers. No Body will lend me or sell me a Pick axe." [124] And in the midst of his voluminous notes on the case appears a poignant exclamation drawn from Juvenal on the handicaps of indigence: "haud facile emergunt. . . ." [125]

Adams' other source of doubt, as his reflections on the Field-Lambert case show, was internal. By studying the classic treatises he hoped to grasp the theory of the law, and by familiarizing himself with the great orators and poets he hoped he might acquire the art of moving the passions of men in a courtroom. In his constant process of self-examination, he searched for at least some faint indications of powers beyond those of others, or what he called "Genius." The purpose of his whole rambling essay on this subject in the Diary Fragment is to see whether he had any flickerings of "Genius" of *any* sort. He was sure he had none of the highest kind—the power to invent "new Wheels, Characters, Experiments, Rules, Laws." [126] But then he asks:

May not Genius [of a different and lesser kind] be shewn in aranging a Mans Diet, Exercise, Sleep, Reading, Reflection, Writing &c. in the best order and Proportion, for His Improvement in Knowledge? ... Patience or a great Superiority to a mans own unsteadiness, is perhaps one of the greatest Marks of Genius. Inatention, Wandering, Unconnected Thoughts, are the opposites to this Patience. [127]

What of his own case? The Diary Fragment is in good part a candid record of his own "Inatention, Wandering, Unconnected Thoughts," and similar "opposites" to the self-discipline he yearned for:

What is the Cause of Procrastination? To day my Stomack is disordered, and my Thoughts of Consequence, unsteady and confused. I cant study to day but will begin tomorrow. Tomorrow comes. Well, I feel pretty well, my head is pretty clear, but Company comes in. . . .
Ballast is what I want, I totter, with every Breeze. My motions are unsteady. . . .
I have so many Irons in the Fire, that every one burns. [128]

From such passages, and from many others like them in the pocket diaries, it is clear that one of Adams' principal motives in keeping a diary was to record his lapses from the ideal regimen that he had set

[124] Same, p. 63.
[125] Below, p. 94.
[126] Below, p. 73.

[127] Below, p. 73.
[128] Below, p. 72, 73, 76.

for himself and that was essential to making the contributions to society that he was determined to make. As his Puritan forebears recorded their spiritual lapses and tremblingly watched for signs of grace, so he looked for signs of progress toward method and accomplishment but commonly could report only lapses from them. In this, as in so many other ways, John Adams told us much about ourselves as he examined and reported on himself.

Harvard Colledge June 8th 1753

8 Friday, at Colledge. a Cloudy, dull morning, and so continu=
:ed till about 5 a Clock, when it began to rain mod=
tely but continued not long, but remained Cloudy all night
= which night I watched with Powers.

9 Saturday. at Colledge, the weather still remaining Cloudy all
Day, till 6 o'Clock, when the Clouds were dissipated, and the
Sun brake forth in all his glory.

10 Sunday, at Colledge a clear morning. heard mr appleton
expound those words in 1. Cor. 12 Chapt. 7 first verses, and
in the afternoon heard him preach from those words in 26
of mathew 41 verse, watch and pray that ye enter not into tempta
tion,

11 monday, at Colledge; a fair morning, and pretty warm
about 2 o'Clock there appeared some symptoms of an appro
ching shower, attended with some thunder, and lightning

12 Tuesday, at Colledge, a Cloudy morning, heard Dr Wigglesworth
preach from the 20 Chapter of exodus 8, 9, & 10th Verses.

13 Wednesday, at Colledge, a Cloudy morning, about 10 o'
Clock the Sun shone out very warm, but about 12 the
heat was, in part, allayed by the rising of the wind.

14 thursday, at Colledge; a Clear, warm, morning but about
2 o'Clock came up a very hard shower, acompanied with some
thunder & lightning —

15 friday, at Colledge, a Clear, warm morning, & so Continued

16 Saturday, at Colledge, a fair morning, but not very warm.

17 Sunday, at Colledge, sunshiny=morning, heard mr
Appleton expound those words in 1. Cor. 12 Chap. from 7.
to the end of 11 verse, in the afternoon heard him preach
from the first Psalm, and first verse. —

18 monday; at Colledge, a warm morning, at 11 o'Clock read
Theses on this question, (viz) antliarum et siphonum pha
nomina solvuntur ex gravitate aeris.

find the Solid Contents of a Sphere.
Rule
Multiply the Diameter by the Circumference, & that Product by the 6th part of the Diameter

John Winthrop was Pro-
fessor of Mathematics and
natural Philosophy at
Harvard College from
1738 to 1779.

was graduated 1732

the Direction of motion is in a direct
Line, drawn to the Centre of the ☉ to wch
it would fall if it's Support were taken away.
A Power is force acting upon a body to move it.
The Intensity of the power is the Great-
ness of the force; two forces acting
Directly contrary Destroy each Other.
Hence in Bodys that move with the same
Velocity, the momenta are as the Velocitys.
Rule. When the Velocitys are un= the
Bodies are un= You must find 2 Quantity[s]
if are to one another as yr masses &
the Velocitys; by multiplying the
Velocities of each Body by it's Mass or
Quantity of matter, & the products will
be to each Other in the Proportion, E, G,
When the Velocity is double & the Mass
stable a double quantity of motion
must be Apply'd Ergo it will be
Sextuple. — When the Velocity in
a Lesser Body, is to yr Velocity in
a Greater Body, as the mass of the
☉ to the mass of the Lesser the
Momenta are =

The Summary of a Course
Of Experimental Philosophical
Lectures, By Mr J. Winthrop.

Lecture I. .... March 10th.

Chapter I.
Definition I.

1. Motion is a Translation from one place
to another & is taken in it's Largest Sense in
Physicks, & upon wt all the Phenomena of
Bodies Depend.
2. The Swiftness of Motion is termed it's
Celerity or Velocity; when a Body moves
swifter than Ordinary, it's said to be
Accelerated, when slower it's said to be
Retarded.
3. The force with wt a Body moves, or the
Quantity of it's motion is call'd it's
Momentum.

Hence we learn the vast Use of Gunpowder
Wch Discharges a 36 pounder with the
same momentum when managed by 3
or 4 men as the Antique Battering Ram,
which took a 1000 men to manage it.
Whence 4 men with the use of Gunpowder
Can do as much Execution against a wall
as a 1000 men with the unweildy
Battering Ram; all wt Appears by
the Exactest Computation ---
The Force by wt bodies are Carried to the
☉ is call'd Gravity. That, in Respect to
a body acted upon by it is call'd the
Weight of the body: the Force of Gravity
Acts = ly & every moment of Time
near the Earths Surface, & the Gravity
in all bodys is proportioned to yr
Quantity of Motion. ---

Lecture 2. March 11th.
All Bodies, Descending Down a plane
Inclined to the Horizon, either Roll or Slide.
The Difference is this, If a perpendicular
let fall from the Center of Gravity, fall
without the Base, the Body will Roll

2. PROFESSOR WINTHROP'S NOTES FOR HIS "COURSE OF . . . LECTURES"
IN NATURAL PHILOSOPHY AT HARVARD

April 1st 1754.

mr Winthrop began a series of Experimental Phylosophy. — and in the 1st place he explaind to us the meaning of nature, and excellence of natural phylosophy which is (he says) the knowledge of those laws by which all the Bodys, in the universe are restrained, it being evident that not only the great masses of matter the heavenly bodys but all the minutest combinations, of matter in each of them are regulated by the same general laws for instance it is plain that all the planets observe exactly the same uniform rules in their revolutions round the sun, that every particle of matter observes on the surface of the earth — as to the usefulness of natural phylosophy, to be convinced of that, it is necessary only to reflect on the state of all the civilized nations of Europe, compared to many nations in affrica who of which natural parts as Europeans, live in a manner very little superiour to the brutes the first Cause, and indeed the alpha & omega of natural phœnomena is motion, their being an utter impossibility that any effect should be produced in a natural way without motion. and this or rather bodies in motion are subject to the following laws, two bodys Different velocitys of swift nights but equal which motion is subject to certain laws which he explained, and I have forgot. But thus much I remember, that this motion is produced by gravity, it was also universally in right lines from the body acted upon by gravity, to the Center of gravity. as the Center of the earth for instance or the other he explaind also, powers weights the line of direction of powers & weights, the Center of gravity, Center of

4. PROFESSOR JOHN WINTHROP, ABOUT 1773,
BY JOHN SINGLETON COPLEY

5. SAMUEL QUINCY, ABOUT 1767,
BY JOHN SINGLETON COPLEY

THE

Religious Philosopher:

Or, the Right USE of

Contemplating the Works

OF THE

CREATOR;

I. In the wonderful Structure of Animal Bodies, and in particular, MAN.
II. In the no less wonderful and wise Formation of the ELEMENTS, and their
various Effects upon Animal and Vegetable Bodies. And,
III. In the most amazing Structure of the HEAVENS, with all its Furniture.

DESIGNED

For the Conviction of ATHEISTS and INFIDELS.

VOL. I.

Throughout which, all the late Discoveries in *Anatomy, Philosophy,* and *Astronomy,* together with the various Experiments made use of to illustrate the same, are most copiously handled by that Learned Mathematician Dr. NIEUWENTYT.

Translated from the LOW-DUTCH,

By JOHN CHAMBERLAYNE, *Esq; F. R. S.*

To which is prefixed,

A LETTER to the TRANSLATOR, by the Reverend *J. T. Desaguliers, LL.D. F. R. S.*

The FOURTH EDITION, Corrected.

Adorned with CUTS.

LONDON:

Printed for J. SENEX in *Fleet-street,* W. INNYS near St. *Paul's,* and J. OSBORN and T. LONGMAN in *Pater-Noster-Row.*
MDCCXXX.

6. JOHN ADAMS' SCIENTIFIC MANUAL AT HARVARD: NIEUWENTIJDT'S "RELIGIOUS PHILOSOPHER"

JOHANNIS VAN MUYDEN
Jcti & Antecessoris

COMPENDIOSA

INSTITUTIONUM

JUSTINIANI

TRACTATIO

In Usum

COLLEGIORUM.

Editio tertia prioribus Auctior & Emendatior

ULTRAJECTI.

Ex Officina GUILIELMI vande WATER, Academiæ Typographi, cIɔ Iɔc ccvII

7. THE GRIDLEY-ADAMS COPY OF VAN MUYDEN'S ABRIDGMENT OF JUSTINIAN'S "INSTITUTES"

To Samuel Quincy

how resolutely, how inviolably, how surprizingly wee have preserved
and pursued the Resolutions wee took of writing each other upon
Points of Law, which we took at Weighmouth! — Oh my friend
how easily wee are find to laudable determinations! but grah
Solon how Soon are such determinations forgot? quite as suddenly as
as the vows of perpetual Constancy made by a young fellow is in the
most violent flurry. — This had some how or other recalled
my Memory a Bit of advice which Polonius gives to his daughter
in Shakespears Hamlet.   I do know

when the blood burns, how prodigal the soul
lends the Tongue vows. These blazes oh my Daughter
giving more light than heat, extinct in both
even in their promise as it is a making
you must not take for Fire.

The Soul is no less Prodigal in lending the Tongue Vows, when the
blood glows with ambition of getting learning & virtue than when it burns
with a very different Passion. The Passion alluded to in these lines. and
...

and whether an Duty & driving away is a Refuge ~~and~~ still are not above
taken up the World we had not folded nor fitted them.

To Crawford

How it is with you I know not but if I am rightly informed I am yet
alive and not dead, and to prove it to you, I will tell you how I
live. I sleep 12 or 13 hours ~~softly~~ Smoke 10 or 12 Pipes, read 5 or 6 pages
think of 19 or 20 Ideas and eat 3 or 4 meals every 24 Hours. ~~you must~~
I have either mounted above or sunk below I have not Penetration enough
to say which, all thought of ~~this~~ Fame Fortune or even Matrimony.
you must not conclude from all this that I am in the Vapours
far otherwise. I never was in much both Health or high Spirits in
my life. both my mind and Body, are in a very easy situation totally
with no Pain, disturbed by no anxiety, and transported with no Pleasure
the strongest desire I have left is of ~~visiting~~ Worcester seeing my friends
at Worcester. ~~but when ever that desire will be gratified I know~~
not — you enjoy in living so near to G— ~~my~~ remind Mr & his Lady
of my sincere friendship. Mr Putnam & his ~~Lady~~, ~~& Mr & his~~
and Kitty Green of the sighs, Wishes Hart Ach, flood tears that in spite
of the vain Boast of Stoical Tranquility, above expresst, continually
attend the Remembrance of her. —

~~~~ let me know ~~er long~~ within this 12 months whether you are
~~cide~~ as I am at this present Writing, and whether you remember one or not
in Letter, either Spare my friends or drown me and my friends together for
will not bear to entertain a fruitless Remembrance of them, after
have quite forgotten me. — ~~Adieu~~, write to me, as soon as you

J. A.

Contemptu Fama, contemni Virtutes. a Contempt of fame generally begets or accompanies a Contempt of Virtue. Iago makes
the Reflection that fame is but breath but vibrated air ~~in empty~~
form. — and ~~Selfish~~ Persons of his Character, are most inclined to
~~make~~ ~~such~~ ~~as~~ feel and express such an indifference about fame
~~wicked~~ Richard, says all men alike to me a loud Vice is like greatness
choose great sins ambition mine! — Some such Reflections & ~~Sense~~ I
suppose I worst men always make to justify or palliate to themselves &
others their own worst Actions — making such a Reflection I think of use
ever a Bone to pick.

Iago. Reputation is an idle and false Imposition, oft got without Merit and
lost without deserving.

10. JOHN ADAMS' BOOK OF SELECTED ORATIONS OF CICERO

11. JOHN ADAMS' DIARY FRAGMENT IN THE TYLER COLLECTION, 1929

The Earliest Diary of John Adams

8 FRIDAY.[1]

At Colledge.[2] A Clowdy, Dull morning, and so continued till about 5 a Clock, when it began to rain m[o]derately But continued not long, But remained Clowdy all night in which night I watched with Powers.[3]

[1] The first day of the first quarter of the 1753–1754 academic year (MH-Ar: Steward's Records, Quarterbill Books, 1720–1756). For a discussion of the impulses and influences leading JA to start a diary record at this time, the beginning of his third or junior sophister year at Harvard, see Introduction, p. 32–34.

[2] During his last three years in college JA lived in the "lowermost northwest chamber" of Massachusetts Hall, then designated as No. 3, subsequently No. 19. In his sophomore year just completed, he shared these quarters with Thomas Sparhawk '55; as both junior and senior sophister he had as his roommate Joseph Stockbridge '55. (MH-Ar: Faculty Records, District Reports, 1st ser., 1752–1755.)

[3] Peter Powers (1728–1800), Harvard 1754, came from Hollis, N.H., and lived in Massachusetts 4; he became the first minister of Newbury, Vt., and, later, of Deer Isle, Maine (Sibley-

Shipton, *Harvard Graduates*, 13:472–478).

The meaning of the phrase "watched with Powers" is susceptible of several interpretations. Commonly, to "watch with" meant to remain awake at the bedside of a sick person (see *OED*). One could also "watch" through a telescope with a fellow student, as JA later remembered doing with his classmate David Sewall "from the Roof of *old* Harvard Colledge [i.e. Hall]" (JA to Benjamin Waterhouse, 17? Aug. 1817, MHi: Adams-Waterhouse Coll.). But since the weather "remained Clowdy all night," this interpretation hardly seems applicable. Finally, there was a local Harvard meaning for "watch," meaning to retain, by permission, a light in one's study for as much as two hours beyond the required 9 P.M. student retiring hour (Morison, *Three Centuries of Harvard*, p. 28).

9 SATURDAY.

At Colledge, the weather still remaining Clowdy all Day, till 6 o'Clock, when the Clowds were Dissipated, and the sun brake forth in all his glory.

10 SUNDAY.

At Colledge a clear morning. Heard Mr. Appleton expound those words in 1. Cor. 12 Chapt. 7 first verses, and in the afternoon heard him preach from those words in 26 of Mathew 41 verse, watch and pray that ye enter not into temptation.[1]

[1] Harvard students attended services on Sundays in the First Church of Cambridge (Morison, *Three Centuries of Harvard*, p. 94). This was a structure built in 1706, since known as "the third meetinghouse," which was replaced in 1756. "Facing the south, it stood on Watch House Hill southwest of the present Lehman Hall" (Hamilton V. Bail, *Views of Harvard: A Pictorial Record to 1860*, Cambridge, 1949, p. 41). Its minister was Rev. Nathaniel Appleton (1693–1784), Harvard 1712 (Sibley-Shipton, *Harvard Graduates*, 5:599–609).

MONDAY [11 JUNE].

At Colledge, a fair morning, and pretty warm. About 2 o'Clock there appeared some symptoms of an approaching shower, attended with some thunder, and lightning.

TUESDAY [12 JUNE].

At Colledge, a Clowdy morning, heard Dr. Wigglesworth Preach from the 20 Chapter of exodus 8, 9 and 10th. Verses.[1]

[1] Morning prayers were said regularly in Holden Chapel in the Yard (Morison, *Three Centuries of Harvard*, p. 94). Rev. Edward Wigglesworth (1693– 1765), Harvard 1710, was Hollis professor of divinity (Sibley-Shipton, *Harvard Graduates*, 5:546–555).

13 WEDNESDAY.

At Colledge, a Cloudy morning, about 10 o'Clock the Sun shone out very warm, but about 12 the heat was, in part, allayed By the rising of the wind.

14 THURDSDAY.

At Colledge, a Clear, warm, morning But about 2 o'Clock came up a very hard shower, acompanied with some thunder and ligh[t]ning.

15 FRYDAY.

At Colledge, a Clear, warm morning, and so Continued.

16 SATURDAY.

At Colledge, a fair morning, but, not very warm.

17 SUNDAY.

At Colledge, sunshiny-morning, heard Mr. Appleton expound those words in 1. Cor. 12 Chap. from 7, to the end of 11 verse, in the afternoon heard him preach from the first Psalm, and first verse.

18 MONDAY.

At Colledge, a warm morning, at 11 'Clock read Theses on this question, (viz) antliarum et siphonum phænomina solvuntur ex gravitate aeris.[1]

[1] "The phenomena of pumps and siphons are explained by the weight of air."

The theses were outlines prepared earlier by tutors or sophisters, generally of single-page length, listing points relevant to the question posed and thus providing material for class discussion. Collections of theses on various questions might be kept by a tutor for the use of succeeding classes or passed down by students. The question might be one which had been disputed at an earlier commencement or be disputed at a future one; for an example see entry of 26 June, below, and note there.

⊰{ 2 }⊱   19 TUESDAY.

At Colledge, a very warm morning, at 11 Disputed on this question (viz) systema Copernicanum est verum mundi systema.[1]

[1] In preparation for the public disputations at commencement, junior and senior sophisters were expected to dispute twice weekly in class. These recitations or exercises in logic were heard by the tutor of the class in his own room, those of the Class of 1755 by Tutor Joseph Mayhew in Massachusetts 5. (Morison, *Three Centuries of Harvard*, p. 25; MH-Ar:Faculty Records, Meeting of 6 March 1752, and District Reports, 1st ser., 1752–1755; entry of 25 June, below.)

20 WEDNESDAY.

At Colledge, a most Charming and Beautifull Scene is this morning displayed. All nature wears a Chearfull garb, after so plentifull a Shower as we were favoured with the Last night, receiving an additionall lustre from the sweet influences of the Sun.—This Day, I (in the religious Phylosopher) read the following experiment, (viz) that the filings of iron, mix'd with sulphur and kneaded to a Dough By the addittion of Cold water will in a few hours Become warm, and at last Be set on fire.[1] Which is undoubtedly true, and if so I think that it affords a very probable method of solving the phænomina of subterraneous fires. For it is highly probable that there are abundance of the particles of iron, Sulphur, and water which, (By the flux of water perhaps in the subterraneous Caverns,) may Be Brought together, and then it appears By the precedent experiment, that this effect (viz a fire) will Be produced. At 2 o'Clock heard Mr. Winthrop's lecture in the Hall, in which he was employed in evincing the sphæroidall form of the earth, which he Did, from the vibrations of pendula, the precession of the æquinox, and from actual mensuration of Degrees at the æquinox and the poles.[2] —After which I extracted the following Hydrostatical Laws from the religious Phylosopher (viz) 1st: if a Body is to be Carried upwards in any liquor, an equall Bulk of said liquor must gravitate or weigh more than such a Body. ⊰{ 3 }⊱ 2ndly. that in order to Cause a Body to sink in a liquor, an equal Bulk of said liquor must weigh less than the Body. 3rdly. if you would have the Body, neither to rise or fall But preserve it's place in any part of the liquor, an equal quantity of the said liquor must weigh equally with the Body.[3]

[1] *The Religious Philosopher: Or, the Right Use of Contemplating the Works of the Creator*, with a detailed outline of its contents on its titlepage (see facsimile in the present volume), was a religio-scientific compilation written by Bernard Nieuwentijdt (1654–1718), translated "from the Low-Dutch" by John Chamberlayne, and published in 3 vols., London, 1718 (*Nieuw Ned. Biog. Woordenboek*, 6:1062–1063). Although by 1750 it was an old-fashioned work, it had gone through numerous French and English translations (BM, *Catalogue*). Its popularity may be succinctly explained by a sentence in the "Letter from the Revd. Mr. Desaguliers" to the translator prefixed to English editions: "He that reads *Niewentyt*, will easily see that a *Philosopher* cannot be an *Atheist*; and if it were true, that a Smattering in *Physics* will give a proud Man a Tincture of *Atheism*, a deep Search into Nature will certainly bring him back to a Religious Sense of God's Wisdom and Providence."

No Adams copy of *The Religious Philosopher* has been found. The iron-and-sulphur experiment JA read this day is in "Contemplation XXI. Of Fire," §24.

[2] On John Winthrop (1714–1779), Harvard 1732, Hollis professor of natural philosophy since 1738 and a scientist of international repute, see *DAB* under his name, and Sibley-Shipton, *Harvard Graduates*, 9:240–264. For his influence on and relations with JA, see the discussion in the Introduction, p. 34–35, above; JA, *Diary and Autobiography*, index; and the JA–Winthrop correspondence in the Adams Papers. As Hollis professor, Winthrop delivered lectures once or twice a week "publicly in the Hall" to "all students that will attend on such topics relating to the science of the mathematics, natural and experimental philosophy as he shall judge most necessary and useful" (*Endowment Funds of Harvard University, June 30, 1947*, Cambridge, 1948, p. 55–56). Winthrop's lecture hall and apparatus room was the west room on the second floor of old Harvard Hall (MH-Ar:Faculty Records, District Reports, 1st ser., 1752–1755, and Papers relating to Harvard Hall, 1672–1764). Copley's portrait of Winthrop beside his telescope is reproduced as an illustration in the present volume.

[3] The precise passage in *The Religious Philosopher* has not been found. JA was evidently abstracting rather than quoting. Nieuwentijdt deals with "Hydrostatical Laws" in "Contemplation XXVI. Of Certain Laws of Nature," §20 *et seq.*

21 THURSDAY.

At Colledge, a warm morning, and Something windy, about Sunset Came up a very hard shower attended with some Thunder, and very Sharp lightning.

22 FRYDAY.

At Colledge, a Charming, pleasant morning, read Dr. Niewentyts Demonstration Co[n]cerning the rays of light emitted from a Burning Candle in a second of time, which he Computes to Be $418660\frac{39}{\vdots}$ Particles.[1]

[1] In *The Religious Philosopher*, "Contemplation XXV. Of the Unspeakable Number, and Unconceivable Smallness of the Particles of which the Universe consists," §16.

23 SATURDAY.

At Colledge, a Clowdy morning, and in the afternoon, Came up a Clowd of thunder and lightning. Towards night fell a very hard shower.

24 SUNDAY.

At Colledge, a Cloudy morning, heard Mr. Cotton of New-town vociferate from the 19. of Proverbs 2nd verse.[1] In the afternoon, from those words in the 37th. Psalm and 4th. verse, Delight thyself in the Lord and he shall give thee thy Desires.

[1] John Cotton (1693–1757), Harvard 1710, had been minister of the church in Newton since 1714; JA's language suggests that Cotton's preaching resembled that of the revivalists he formerly admired (Sibley-Shipton, *Harvard Graduates*, 5:517–524).

25. MONDAY.

At Colledge, a very rainy, morning, at 11 o'Clock Disputed from the question assigned us last tuesday But on which we Did not then Dispute By reason of Mr. Mayhews Being employed in taking an account of the Books and other things, Contained in the Library in order to the Printing a new Catalogue thereof.[1]

[1] Joseph Mayhew (1710–1782), Harvard 1730, tutor to the Class of 1755, had served as tutor since 1739 and fellow of the Corporation since 1742 (Sibley-Shipton, *Harvard Graduates*, 8:730–734). It was he who administered JA his examination for entrance to Harvard, as described in a famous and charming passage in JA's *Diary and Autobiography*, 3:259–260.

When in 1753 John Rand '48 succeeded Stephen Badger '47 as keeper of the College library in old Harvard Hall, Mayhew, along with Tutors Belcher Hancock '27 and Thomas Marsh '31, had been appointed to receive an account from Badger "of the present state of the sd. Library and make report of it to the Corporation" (MH-Ar:Corporation Records, Meeting of 21 May 1753). Their "exact survey of the library" or inventory of the books which are "actually in it, which are absent but charged, and also such as are absent and not charged, and also an account of the rarities which are there and which belong to it but are not now to be found there," was not submitted to the Cor-

poration until the spring of 1754, when they were allowed special compensation of 30s. and an advertisement was ordered placed requiring the return of valuable books that the survey revealed had been for a long time in the hands of individuals (same, Meeting of 1 April 1754). The advertisement appeared in the *Boston Evening-Post* for 8 April, p. 2, col. 1, and probably in other papers.

No printed catalogue of the Harvard Library for the 1750's is known. The official records do not, in fact, suggest an intention to use the current inventory for such a purpose. The last printed library catalogue was that of 1735 (actually a second supplement to that of 1723), and no later one was issued until 1773. Since the library was consumed in the fire that destroyed old Harvard Hall in 1764, the only record available of books which were in the library while JA was an undergraduate (beyond those in the 1723 catalogue and its supplements) is Andrew Eliot's compilation of books in the hands of sophisters at the time of the fire (MH-Ar).

26 TUESDAY.

At Colledge, a very rainy Day, as it has remained since yesterday-morning. By reason of my illness omitted Disputing from this question, generalia æstuum phænomina solvuntur ab atractione solis et lunæ.[1]

[1] "The general phenomena of the tides are explained by the attraction of the sun and moon." This "quæstio" had been one of the "Theses Physicæ" disputed at commencement in 1746 and would be again at JA's commencement in 1755. See entry of 18 June, above, and note there; MH-Ar:Theses and Quæstiones, 1737–1810.

{4}   27 WEDNESDAY.

At Colledge. A Clowdy morning. Afternoon, together with Lock,[1] took a ride to Watertown-Bridge and from thence round through Brookline Back to Colledge again.[2]

[1] Samuel Locke (1732–1778), of Lancaster, Harvard 1755, later minister at Sherborn and, from 1770 to 1773, a most ill-fated president of Harvard College (Sibley-Shipton, *Harvard Graduates*, 13:620–627; see also JA, *Diary and Autobiography*, 3:260).

[2] The route from Cambridge to Brookline would under normal conditions have been across "the Great Bridge over *Charles-River* in *Cambridge*," built in 1662–1663 and located "at the foot of Brighton Street [now Boylston Street]" (Mass., *House Jour.*, 29:99; Lucius R. Paige, *History of Cambridge, Massachusetts*, 1630–1877, Boston, 1877, p. 195). A petition to the General Court in Dec. 1752, however, indicates that the bridge "received such a Shock the last Winter by the Ice" that "a thorough Repair" became an "abso-

lute Necessity" (Mass., *House Jour.*, 29:99). On 2 July 1753 the *Boston Evening-Post* gave notice: "*Whereas the great Bridge in* Cambridge *has for some Time past been out of Repair, so that there was no passing over it;* This is to inform the Publick, that the said Bridge is now so far repaired, that Chairs, Chaises, and other Carriages may pass over it with Safety."

The bridge in Watertown, also known as the "great Bridge," was built in 1718–1719 and crossed the Charles River near the present Watertown Square at Galen Street (*Watertown Records*, Watertown and Newton, Mass., 1894–1939, 2:256–257, 261, 263; G. Frederick Robinson and Ruth Robinson Wheeler, *Great Little Watertown: A Tercentenary History*, Watertown, Mass., 1930, p. 48).

28. THURSDAY.

At Colledge, a Clowdy-Day.

29 FRYDAY.

At Colledge, a Clear morning. Heard the valedictory oration, pronounced, By Oliver.[1] 2 o Clock set out for Boston, Designing to go from thence home.

[1] Attendance at exercises being required of all students other than those in the graduating class until 1 July, and senior sophisters not being allowed, while preparing for their "sitting solstices" or oral examinations, to leave Cambridge between 21 March and 1 July (MH-Ar: Corporation Records, College Book No. 7, Meeting of 21 May 1753), the last recitation day before 1 July became the appropriate time for a meeting in Hall. On this occasion, attended by the Presi-

dent and Fellows, speakers from the senior class, including a valedictorian chosen by his classmates, would perform (Morison, *Three Centuries of Harvard,* p. 119). Between this precursor of "class day" and commencement (in 1753 on 18 July) there seem to have been no regular recitations, though the formal summer vacation of six weeks did not begin until after commencement day.

Thomas Oliver (1734–1815), identified by JA as valedictorian for his class, also received Faculty appointment as orator at the morning exercises of commencement in 1753 (MH-Ar:Theses and Quæstiones, 1753, handwritten notation). On him see Sibley-Shipton, *Harvard Graduates,* 13:336–344, and an article by Oliver Elton, Col. Soc. Mass., *Pubns.,* 28 (1935):37–66.

29 [JUNE 1753–JANUARY 1754?].[1]

Sat out from Boston, home where having tarried 7, or 8 Days I set out on a journey together with Mr. Adams to Piscataqua, to which I went By way of Litchfeild, going firstly from Boston over Charlston-ferry through Charlestown, Mistick, Menotomy, Lexington, Bedford, Bilerica, Chensford, Dracut to which I passed from Chensford over the river. From Dracut I proceeded to Nottingham, Londonderry, Hamstead, Kingston, Kensington, Hampton, Greenland, Newington where having tarried about a fortnight and vizitted Portsmouth, I returned home and at the appointed time return'd to Colledge where I have been ever since, save that I went home once for a fortnight.[2]

[1] As initially dated by the diarist, this is a *second* entry for 29 [June 1753], but being actually a collective entry for all the rest of the year, it was of course set down much later than the date left at the head. The latest possible date for its composition would seem to be 2 Jan. 1754, the beginning of the winter vacation mentioned in the next entry in the Diary Fragment. It could, however, have been written as early as 28 Dec. 1753. The chronology appears to be as follows: JA returned to Cambridge at the end of the six-week summer vacation on 29 Aug., remaining there during the rest of this first quarter and during all of the second, i.e. until 13 December. From the Steward's records it is possible to pinpoint the two-week absence of which JA speaks in the present entry (twenty-one days each half-year were allowed without penalty) as having been taken at the beginning of the third quarter, namely 14–28 Dec., for the assessments against him for commons and sizings during this quarter were only £0 10s. 5¼d. as compared, for example, with £2 16s. 0¾d. during the second quarter (MH-Ar:Steward's Quarterbill Books).

This collective entry is the first in the Diary Fragment showing the characteristics of JA's "experimental" handwriting, described and discussed in the Introduction and illustrated by a facsimile page in the present volume. These characteristics persist in the later entries in 1754 and then disappear from the Fragment.

[2] Nearly seventy years after he wrote this matter-of-fact and tantalizingly brief entry recording what may have been his first trip of any extent away from home, JA furnished from memory a much more detailed and colorful account of it. This was in one of a series of reminiscences of their undergraduate days at Harvard exchanged in letters between JA and his only surviving classmate, David Sewall of York, Maine, running from Nov. 1821 through Jan. 1822 that are of the highest interest despite the fallibility of old men's memories. In his letter of 14 Dec. 1821 Sewall enclosed a diverting narrative of a journey from Cambridge to Portsmouth that he had taken in June 1754 (while he was still an undergraduate) in company with the venerable and eccentric Harvard tutor Henry Flynt (Adams Papers; the enclosure,

filed separately under 1754, was communicated by CFA and printed in MHS, *Procs.*, 1st ser., 16 [1878]:5–11). In replying, JA wrote:

"Your journey has brought to my recollection one of my own made two or three years [actually one year] before yours. I went with a young preacher Ebenezer Adams the son of that uncle [i.e. JA's uncle, Rev. Joseph Adams] up through Chelmsford, to London Derry and a place beyond it called Litchfield if I remember right and from thence down through Kensington to Newington and Portsmouth. Either going or returning we visited Parson Whipple whose lady persecuted me as much as she did afterwards father F[lynt]. The lady had a fine figure and a fair face. At dinner I was very bashful and silent. After dinner Parson W. invited us into another [room] where he took a pipe himself and offered us pipes. I was an old smoker and readily took one. The [word torn away] lady very soon came into the room, lifted up her hands and cried out in a masculine voice, I am astonished to see that pretty little boy with a pipe in his mouth smoking that nasty poisoned tobacco. I cant bear the sight. I was as bashful and timorous as a girl, but I resented so much being called a little boy at 15 or 16 years of age and as stout as her husband, that I determined not to be frightened out of my pipe so I continued to puff away. You may well suppose that I bore no very good will to that lady till I afterward became acquainted with the character of Miss Hannah Whipple who afterwards married Dr. Bracket and gave two thousand dollars to the botanical garden [in] Cambridge. The excellences of that daughter very early atoned for all the severity of the mother and I have long since esteemed her an amiable and intelligent woman though sometimes a little too free with her guests. I recollect nothing more worth recording in my tour except that we called at Parson Bridges at Chelmsford and Parson Fogs at Kensington where we had much conversation respecting Mr. Wibert afterwards my minister then much celebrated for the elegance of his style." (24 Dec. 1821, FC in an amanuensis' hand, writ-

ten on blank pages of Sewall's letter to JA, 14 Dec. 1821, Adams Papers.)

From JA's two accounts the itinerary of his vacation trip can be pretty satisfactorily reconstructed. He had left Cambridge on 29 June, "tarried" about a week at home in Braintree, then set out from Boston at the end of the first week in July with his cousin, Rev. Ebenezer Adams (1726–1767), Harvard 1747, to visit JA's uncle and Ebenezer's father, Rev. Joseph Adams (1689–1783), Harvard 1710, the veteran minister of Newington, N.H., a village on the south side of the Piscataqua River immediately above Portsmouth. They crossed the Charles River basin by ferry to Charlestown and the Mystic River to "Mistick" (Medford), and went on through "Menotomy" (later West Cambridge and now Arlington), Lexington, Bedford, and Billerica to Chelmsford. Crossing the Merrimack to Dracut in the extreme northeastern corner of Middlesex co., they followed the river through the New Hampshire villages of Nottingham West and Litchfield, where they turned northeast and passed through Londonderry, Hampstead, Kingston, Hampton Falls, and Greenland to Newington, spent a fortnight there, and visited the little maritime metropolis of Portsmouth.

The return journey was by the same or a very similar route, for the only precise date in the trip as a whole that can be established is that of their visit, in returning, with "Parson" Ebenezer Bridge (1716–1792), Harvard 1736, at Chelmsford. Bridge recorded in his Diary on 27 July: "Mr. Ebz. Adams a Preacher and Mr. Adams a Student at Har. Col. visited and dined with me" (MS, MH). The other stops mentioned in JA's letter to Sewall could have been made "Either going or returning." At Kensington, they called on Rev. Jeremiah Fogg (1712–1789), Harvard 1730, where conversation about Rev. Anthony Wibird (1729–1800) was natural because JA's cousin Ebenezer and Wibird were classmates and both preaching at Amesbury about this time. The little tiff over JA's smoking occurred at Hampton Falls in the home of Rev. Joseph Whipple (1701–1757), Harvard 1720, whose wife, the former Elizabeth Cutts, was old enough to be JA's mother, which helps explain what JA thought was highhandedness on her part toward him. He was mistaken, however (as Sewall pointed out in a later letter), in supposing that Hannah Whipple, who married Dr. (and Judge) Joshua Brackett in 1760 and became a benefactress of botanical study at Harvard, was the daughter of Parson Whipple and his wife. Hannah Whipple came from Kittery, Maine. (See Sewall to JA, 18 Jan. 1822, Adams Papers.)

Sketches of all the men concerned are included in Sibley-Shipton, *Harvard Graduates*: of Ebenezer Adams at 12:103; Joseph Adams, 5:502–506; Brackett, 13:197–201; Bridge, 10:17–27; Fogg, 8:710–714; Sewall, 13:638–645; Whipple, 6:415–417; Wibird, 12:226–230. On the two Adamses see also Adams Genealogy.

[FEBRUARY 1754.]

This winter, we had a vacation.[1]

In the winter of 1754 we had no snow at all save a smattering or two, But perpetuall rains and warm weather thro'ought the whole.[2]

[1] In the academic year 1752–1753 there had been no winter vacation at the College. This was because during 1752 the number of instructional days had been greatly diminished, in the spring by the closure necessitated by a smallpox epidemic, in the fall by the loss of eleven days (3–13 Sept.) through the Act of Parliament in 1751 (24 Geo. 2, c. 23) providing for a change from the Julian to the Gregorian calendar in 1752. From 22 April all college exercises, including commencement, had therefore been suspended, not to be resumed until 14 (i.e. 3, old style) September.

Moreover, the permanence of the vacation on the College calendar was in some doubt. A winter vacation of five weeks beginning the first Wednesday in January had been authorized in 1749 and renewed for a further trial period of three years in 1751. Upon the expiration of that period the Overseers refused to accept the Corporation's vote for a further extension of five years and approved a continuance only "for the year current." In 1754 the vacation period was from 2 Jan. to 6 February. (MH-AR:Corporation Records, College Book No. 7; Overseer's Records 1744–1768; Meetings of 1 Oct. 1751, 4 May, 3 Oct. 1752, 1 Oct. 1754).

[2] JA's recollection of the weather during recent months is confirmed in a general way by the daily meteorological observations in Professor John Winthrop's Meteorological Journal, 1742–1759 (MS, MH-Ar). He records snow on two days in January and one day in February, none heavy, and "a little" snow on three days in February. There were rains on nine days in January and seven days in February. The Fahrenheit thermometer reached a high of 54° in January, 52.5° in February. The low was 3° in January, 12° in February. The mean morning and afternoon readings, 29°–38°, were somewhat higher than in immediately preceding years.

MARCH [1754].

Beg[inning *of March*]. Had a small flurry of snow.[1]

[1] There was snow in Cambridge on 2 March and "a little" on 7 March (John Winthrop, Meteorological Journal, MH-Ar). Other considerations rather favor the 2d over the 7th of March as the precise date of this entry in the Diary Fragment.

MARCH 8TH.[1]

A Clowdy morning. I am now reading my lord Orrerys letters to his son Concerning Dr. Swift and his writings, which for softness and delicacy of style, accuracy and serenity of sentiment, are absolutely inimitable.[2] Reading also the last volume of Monsieur Rollin's Belles Lettres which are worth their weight in gold.—for his excellent reflections on every remarkable event that occurs in history he informs his readers of the true source ⋅{ 5 }⋅ of every action and instructs them in the method of forming themselves upon the models of virtue to be met with in History.[3]

[1] The first day of the fourth quarter of the academic year 1753–1754 (MH-Ar:Steward's Records, Quarterbill Books).

[2] *Remarks on the Life and Writings of Dr. Jonathan Swift . . . in a Series of Letters from John Earl of Orrery to His Son, the Honourable Hamilton Boyle,* London, 1751, was the work of John Boyle, 5th Earl of Orrery (1717–1762), a friend of Swift, Pope, and Johnson and the author of miscellaneous literary works (*DNB*). "[A]s the first attempt at an account of Swift," it "attracted much attention" (same); but modern estimates of its authority and style fall far short of JA's enthusiasm for Orrery's book.

[3] The faulty punctuation of this passage on Rollin follows that of the MS precisely.

Charles Rollin (1661–1741), rector of the University of Paris, was the author and compiler of numerous historical and pedagogical works that, in translation, were extraordinarily popular in England and America for many years and notably so in the Adams family. See *Adams Family Correspondence,* 1:142–143, where the known Adams copies of Rollin's works are listed. See also JA's commendation of Rollin's *Method of Teaching and Studying the Belles Lettres* in a letter to AA, 7 July 1776, and a facsimile of the titlepage of that work (same, 2:40–41, and facing p. 263).

[17? MARCH 1754.]

Kept sabath at Cambridge. March about the middle.

MARCH 18TH.

In the Evening we had several very sharp flashes of lightning, attended with a Distant grumbling of thunder.

19 [MARCH 1754].

This morning is beyond description, Beautyfull, the Skie bespangled with Clouds which shed a lustre on us by the refraction of the rays of light, together with the healthy and enlivening air, which was purifyed By the thunder, afford most spirited materials for Contemplation.[1] The gaiety of the weather is equally delightfull to the phylosopher, Poet and the man of Pleasure. The Phylosopher finds his passions all Calm, serene, and Pliable so that he finds no Difficulty in subjecting them to the subserviency of his reason, he can now contemplate all the gaudy appearances of nature and like Pythagoras bring Phylosophy down from heaven and make her conversible to men. The Poet thinks this the Best time to Converse with his muse and

Consequently gives himself up wholly to her directions. His whole soul is at her disposall and he no more retains the government of himself. While the man of pleasure find such delicacys arising from the objects of sence as are adapted to produce the highest sensations of delight in him.[2]

[1] "Rain in the night. Fair with clouds" (John Winthrop, Meteorological Journal, MH-Ar).

[2] Here a blank space of nearly half a page appears in the MS, and here also the writing in JA's experimental hand of 1754–1756 ends, though temporarily. The following three pages in the MS (i.e. {6–8}) were also originally left blank by the diarist except for the canceled beginning of his notes on Winthrop's lectures (first entry of 1 April 1754, below). The editors suppose that JA intended to fill up this space with journal entries for the rest of March. See note 1 on the following entry and Introduction, p. 8.

{6} [ON THE LAW OF NATURE AND THE MORAL SENSE AMONG ANIMALS AND AMONG MEN, OCTOBER–DECEMBER 1758.][1]

Q[uery]. Has any Species of Animals, besides Mankind, ever given Proofs that they have any idea of Justice, of R[igh]t or Wrong. That they have any Discernment of the Difference between Actions and Characters? Have they any moral Sense?

Q. Have they any sense of the Advantages of Temperance and of the Disadvantages of the Contrary. Will not horses, when they are hot, drink large Quantities of Water without Regret and frequently Chestfounder themselves so? They seem to have very little Concern or Apprehension about the Consequences of Violent Exercise and plentiful Eating and drinking.

Q. Did the[2] Jewish Law that oxen, and Horses, that pushed or kicked a Man to death, or that copulated with any man or woman, should be slain, stand on this Principle, that the Brutes knew the Prohibitions they were under and were accountable, for the Breach of them?

Q. Let me examine, when, and how this Notion of a Law common to Beasts and men, arose in the World, and in what sense it was understood.

Q. If there are Rules of Justice, of Morality, that extend to all Animals, what do those Men deserve, who have believed this and yet plundered, preyed upon, Murdered Fowl, Beasts and fishes in all Ages.—How can we answer for robbing the Birds Nests of their Eggs and Young, for butchering, fleecing, Sheep, Lamb's, Calves, Oxen &c., or will the Assistance we give them, in providing Food and shelter for them in Winter, and Pasturage in Winter [*i.e.* summer?], justify our

Cruel Depredations upon them?—But we never feed or Clothe Robbins, ⟨*wild Geese*⟩ wild fowl &c. What Justice then, in killing them? Is it not Murder?

Q. ⟨*Self Love and*⟩ Self Preservation, and the Desire of Propagation, are common to all Animals. But the Law of Nature, which teaches other Species to nurse their Young, teaches man to imbue the tender Minds of Children, with Knowledge and Virtue.

Q. The Law of Nature, as an Instinct is perhaps common, but the Institutions which Reason adds to Instinct, are peculiar to man. Now Justice, Temperance, Gratitude, Benevolence, &c. are Institutions of Reason, are found and proved to be human Duties, and beneficial to society, by Reason and Experience.

Jus naturale est quod Natura omnia Animalia docuit, Jus enim istud non est humani Generis proprium, sed omnium Animalium, quæ, aut in terra, aut in mari aut in Cœlo nascuntur.[3]

Temperance, Prudence, Justice, and Fortitude.

Jus naturale, is omnium Animalium.

Is the Law of Nature, common to all Animals, from Man the Lord of all, down to the smallest Animalcules, discernible by Glasses?

Are all the Rules of natural Law, which men are obliged to observe, incumbent upon all Birds, Beasts, fishes.

Temperance, Prudence, Justice, and Fortitude, are Duties of the Law of human Nature. But have the Beasts and Birds and Fishes, given any Proofs that they have any Idea of these Virtues? any sense of their obligation to Practise them? Do they not gorma[n]dize, do ⟨*they not*⟩ what Prudence, do they not rob, each other. Are not many of them timorous, afraid of Trifles and shadows? But their Vices are no Proof that they are not under these Laws, more than human Vices will prove that Men are not.—We do not understand their Language, their signs, nor their sounds enough to know, what Knowledge they have of their own Constitutions, and Connections.[4] But is this Question worth a [...] Discussion?—I have no concern with a society of Birds or Beasts or fishes, or Insects. I shall neither be [concerned?] for nor against the Cattle. The Law of Nature includes the Laws of Reason as much as Self Love and Desire of Propagation and education, includes those Rules of Temperance, Prudence, Justice, and Fortitude which Reason, by the help of Experience, discovers to be productive of the ⟨*good*⟩ Happiness and Perfection of human [Nature?].

[1] The entry which follows is in JA's small and sometimes almost indecipherable hand familiar in his Diary and correspondence from the latter part of 1756 on. Having left three pages blank after his entry of 19 March 1754 (see note on that entry, preceding), he afterward economically filled them up, no

doubt at about the same time that he wrote the later entries in the Diary Fragment, which are in the same hand and unquestionably belong to the last three months of 1758, or, at the latest, the first week or so of Jan. 1759.

² MS: "they."

³ "Natural law is taught by Nature to all living things, for that law appertains not only to the human species but to all living things that are born in the earth, sea, or sky." Source not identified, but compare the phrasing in Justinian's *Institutes*, bk. 2, title 1, § 12, as quoted by JA in his *Legal Papers*, 2:73.

⁴ Possibly "Conventions."

‹7›   APRIL 1ST. 1754.

⟨Then, Mr. Winthrop began a Course of Experimental⟩ ¹

¹ Written in JA's experimental hand of 1754–1756, with this fragmentary line canceled and the date heading certainly intended to be. This false beginning of JA's notes on Winthrop's lectures heads p. ‹7› of the MS and was lined out, presumably at once, because

JA supposed that he would need more space than he had left for his ⟨unwritten⟩ journal entries for the last dozen days of March; see note on entry of 19 March 1754, above. For the true beginning of the lecture notes, see the second entry of 1 April 1754, p. 60, below.

[NOTES ON CIVIL LAW, DECEMBER 1758–JANUARY 1759.]¹

Sequestration is when two, or more, deposit a controverted Thing, with a 3d Person, on that Condition, that he, at the Conclusion of the suit, Dispute, will restore the Thing to the Conqueror.² This is either voluntary, which is ⟨made⟩ done by the Agreement of Parties, or necessary, which is done by the Authority of a Judge. This, regularly, is prohibited. From a Deposit, arises a twofold Action, direct and contrary. A direct Action of detinue, is a personal Action of good Faith, famous, public, which is given [. . .] to the Deponent against the Depositary, ⟨to⟩ for this, viz. that he may restore the thing deposited, sarcio, to repair, mend, and repair the Damage given by fraud and faults committed. Lata Culpa, by a gross fault. A contrary Action is given to the Depositary against the Deponent, to be saved harmless.

A Pawn or Pledge is a Contract of the Law of Nations, of good faith, re constans, consisting in a thing, fact, by what means, in what Ways, an Obligation ⟨to⟩ Contract, in fact by a fact, an Action or Deed, consisting in fact, in a Thing, by which any Thing is given to a Creditor by a Debtor or [any other?] ⟨for a⟩ as a Security of his Debt, on that Condition that the same Thing be restored, in Specie, on the Payment of the Debt. Soluto Debito, the Debt being paid, eadem res in Specie. From this Contract, arises an Action, direct and contrary. The direct Action ⟨of a Pl⟩ for a Pawn is given to the Debtor, on Payment of the Debt, against the Creditor, for this, that he restore the Pawn with all Cause, and repair the Damage, given by fraud, or by any gross or even by a light fault. Levis culpa, a light fault. A Contrary Action is given to the Creditor, against a Debtor, to be saved harmless.

55

Of the Performance of fraud, of fault, and Accident. Præstare. To answer for a fraud or fault is to repair the Damage, given by Deceit, by Accident or by fault. Deceit is all subtilty, Deceit, or Contrivance, employed to circumvent, deceive, or delude another. A fraud is all subtilty, Deceitfulness, or Contrivance, employed to circumvent, deceive, delude another. A fault is nothing less than Negligence [...], whether of omission or Commission, in the Affairs of another, and is T[hree]fold gross, light and lightest. A gross fault is not to use that dilligence which even a negligent father of a family uses, or to be ignorant of what all understand. This in Contracts is compared to Deceit, fraud, excepting the Case of a Capital Crime. A light fault is not to use that diligence which a thrifty and diligent father of a family, uses in his own Things. This fault is regularly meant, denoted when the Word faults is put simply in the Laws. The lightest fault is not to adhibit, use, employ, exert that diligence, which a most diligent father of a family exerts. An accidental Misfortune is a greater Strength, to which human Weakness is not able to resist. Humana, Casus fortuitus, a casual Mishap. A Chance medly. [...] Dolum. To answer for a fraud. Fraud is answered for, paid for, repaid in all Contracts. Accidents, misfortune in none, except in Lending, Loan. Loan. Payment of what is not due, is in some respects like a Loan, which nevertheless is not a true Contract but a sort of Contract, by which he who received what was [undue?] is obliged to him, who by Error and Ignorance paid what was [...] that it be [...].[3] A fault, regularly, is made good, repaid, according to these 3 Rules. 1. As often as a ⟨Contract⟩ Bargain is driven, a Contract is taken, entered into, for the Sake of the giver alone, so often Deceit only and a gross fault is answered for, as in a Deposit. 2. As often as a Contract is celebrated, for the sake of the receiver alone, so often fraud, deceit, fault, even the lightest is answered for as in [commodatum].[4] A direct Action of [...] is a personal civil Action, demanding a Thing, which is given to a Lender against the Borrower to restore the Thing lent in Specie, and answer for fraud and [...] the light fault.[5] 3. As often as the Utility, Advantage, Benefit of both, takes place in a Contract, so often fraud, a gross and a light fault, is answered for, as in a Pawn, Buying and selling. The aforesaid Rules concerning fraud, Negligence and Misfortune, then cease, if the contractors otherwise agree; except if it is agreed that fraud shall not be answered, even when any special Reason shall except this or that Contract from the common Rules.

Of the Obligations of Words. An Obligation of Words, or any Stipulation, is a Contract of the civil Law, of strict law, consisting in

Words, by which he, who is asked, whether he is about to give [or to do?] what he is interrogated, answers. Emancipation is an Act by which Children are dismiss[ed] from the father's Power. Act.[6] From a Stipulation arises a two fold Action, a personal Action of a certain Thing; if a certain Thing is drawn into a Stipulation and of an uncertain Thing, or an Action, from a Bargain, if an uncertain Thing is drawn into a Stipulation. Each is a personal Action, civil, of strict Law, which is given to the stipulant, against the Promisor to oblige him to perform what he promised.

Every Stipulation is either pure, or for a certain day, or conditional. A pure Stipulation is one which is contracted without [the addition?] of any time or Condition, and in that pure Stipulation, the Day of the Obligation begins, and comes immediately. The Day of the Obligation is said to proceed when a Thing, drawn into Obligation, begins to be due, altho it cannot yet be demanded. A day is said to come when that can be demanded which is due. A stipulation, at a certain day, is that which is [made] annexing a day, appointing a day, in which the Money is to be paid. A day may be added to an Obligation 2 Ways, either as a Time from which, as after 5 years I will give, or as a Time to which, as untill 5 years, or as long as I shall live. In the 1st Case, the day of the Obligation, immediately [goes?] but comes not before the day exists. It is [right?] however for the Debtor to pay before the day if he will. In the other Case also, the time being past, the Obligation is perpetuated by the Law it self, but the Promissor of the Agreement, by the Exception of the Agreement [...] may [...] himself. The time moreover may be added to the Stipulation not only expressly, but also it is sometimes tacitly implied; which happens if a Place is added to the Stipulation, the Performance it self of the Thing, or fact in it self against a space of Time. A conditional stipulation is, one which is made, with regard to a future, [uncertain?] Case, in that the day of the Obligation, neither goes nor comes, unless the Condition happens. Yet the Hope of the future Obligation is transmitted, from the Part of each Contractor to his Heirs. [But?] if the Condition is affixed to the present or the past time, that is scarcely esteemed a [Contract?] nor differs the Obligation.

⁅8, *upside down*[7]⁆ A Stipulation is made in any Tongue yet the Question and Answer must agree, and, all things [...] drawn into that, which are in Commerce, also the facts must be possible and lawful, [...] own, not [anothers?]. If a fact is drawn into [...] in a Stipulation, the Promissor cant be compelled precisely to the fact, but is freed from [...] and therefore it is [actible?] to [...][8] Stipulator, for thus he exempts himself from the difficulty of proving that which is due.

Of the 2 Parties of stipulating and promising. The [accessors] of the Stipulation are 2 Stipulators to each of whom the same Thing, Speech by [...] is [promised?] in the whole. The [Accessor?] of promising or of owing the [joint?] Promisers or [...] conjuncta oratione. Fellow Promisers, joint Promisers [...]⁹ 2 [promisors?] who singly promise the same Thing, at one time, to a Person Stipulating. Stipulans, in eadem Res, the en solidum, the same thing to a [...]. Eandem Rem, in solidum. That therefore 2 may be joint Accessers to [...] of Stipulating or promising, it is required 1. that the same Thing be draw[n] into the stipulation, brought into the Stipulation. 2. That the Promise be made from one and the same Cause. 3. That the whole be promised to both, and by both. Yet one of the Accessors may be rightly obliged, purely, and the other, on Condition, or to a certain day. The Effect of such a stipulation is, that the 2 Partners may act or agree, for the whole, singly, separately, yet so that one accepting, receiving a Debt, or one paying the whole Obligation is destroyed. But if joint Debtors are obliged to any thing by an alternate Engagement, they may enjoy the Benefit [of the] Divisons. Of the Stipulation of Servants. Even servants may stipulate from the Person of their Masters, also an hereditary servant, and a common servant. But a servant acquires not any thing that is stipulated to himself, but to his Master or to the Inheritance or if there are many Masters he stipulates to each for Part, unless it was by the Order of one, or for one by name. Yet a servant, if he stipulates for a fact, acquires it to himself. Of the Division of Stipulation. [...] Stipulations are either, judicial, or prætorial, or conventional, or common.¹⁰

¹ The text of this entry is written in JA's small but familiar hand, immediately following the canceled beginning of his notes on Winthrop's lectures, preceding, on a page of the MS otherwise left entirely blank in 1754. For the assigned date see the following note.

² This is the beginning of JA's notes on Johannes van Muyden's *Tractatio* ..., 3d edn., Utrecht, 1707, an abridgment of Justinian's *Institutes*, which had been lent to him by Jeremy Gridley in Oct. 1758, which JA read during the following months, and which he later obtained for his own library from the sale of Gridley's books. See the Introduction, p. 15–16, and references there; see also the titlepage of the Gridley-JA

copy of the *Tractatio* (now in MB) as reproduced in the present volume. JA's notes in this entry are drawn from p. 114–121 of Van Muyden, beginning in the *Institutes* at bk. 3, part way through title 15, and continuing part way through title 19. Since JA is known to have resumed his reading of this work on 20 Dec. 1758 at p. 99 (*Diary and Autobiography*, 1:63), we may suppose the present notes were written late in Dec. 1758 or early in Jan. 1759.

It cannot be said that JA was an exemplary note-taker. He not only omitted author, title, and all references to sections and pages of the book he was abstracting, but seems to have been satisfied at times with gibberish. His writing is so cramped and his translation so rough that sometimes, even with the Latin original in hand, it has proved impossible to render his words and grasp his meaning.

³ The preceding four lines, beginning with the word "Loan" as repeated, are out of context; they are possibly from some source cited in Van Muyden's marginal gloss.

⁴ Omitted in JA's notes; supplied from Van Muyden's text.

⁵ The preceding sentence is out of context; see note 3.

⁶ This word and the whole sentence preceding it are out of context; see note 3.

⁷ The notes that follow in this entry are upside down on p. ⧏ 8 ⧐ of the MS, below the passage we have entitled Rules for Determining the Excellence of a Language (next entry in the Diary Fragment). It may therefore be presumed that *all* the notes on Van Muyden were written later than the "Rules."

⁸ Five or six words undecipherable.

⁹ Two or three words undecipherable.

¹⁰ JA's notes on Van Muyden continue without a break much later in the MS; see p. 100, below.

⧏ 8 ⧐ [RULES FOR DETERMINING THE EXCELLENCE OF
A LANGUAGE, OCTOBER–DECEMBER 1758.]¹

What are the Rules, Criteria, to determine the Merit or Excellence of a Language?—Suppose you was to examine, which was the best, and which the worst of the Languages, Greek, Latin, french and English? How would you decide.

One Excellence of a Language, is Conciseness. That Language is to be preferred in which Ideas and Thoughts may be clearly conveyed to the Hearer or Reader in the fewest Words.—But Q. whether Conciseness is not a Property, a Talent of the Writer rather than of the Language. Would Dean Swift if he had been as great Master of french as he was of English, have expressed himself as concisely as he has in English?—Some Languages have Technical Words to express certain Collections of Ideas, that cannot be expressed, in another, without a Periphrasis. A Man may write more concisely, in french on fortification and Gunnery, and Cookery and Dancing, than he can in English. In Italian, upon Musick, Statuary, Painting, than in any other. In Greek on Anatomy, Physick &c.

2. Copiousness, i.e. Variety of Words to express the same Idea. For as Eloquence and Poetry, are wrote in Measure, feet, Numbers, often times a Dissillable or a Trissilable will be wanted to round a Period, or compleat a Line. Now, if there is a Monasyllable, and a Dissillable or a Trissillable, in the same Language to express the same Idea, the Writer or Speaker may select that which fits his Measure. Another Advantage of Variety of Words is this. When one Word cannot be so easily or emphatically pronounced, after another, out of several one may be chosen, that will exactly answer.

3. A proper Distribution of Consonants and Vowells, that a Language may neither be effeminately soft, nor brutally rough and grating to the Ear.

4. A Connection [or] Analogy between the sound of the Words and the Things signified by them. Thus, the great and sublime Objects should be signified by Words of a loud grand sound. Slow Actions should be expressed by slow heavy Words. But quick swift Actions by Words that require, and occasion an impetuous Pronunciation.

5. As one considerable Design of Poetry and Eloquence is to move the Passions, a similarity between the sound of Words separately or in Combination and the Passions of the mind. For there is a peculiar sound to every one of the Passions.—These Hints may lead me into a large field of Speculation and Inquiry.

Inference. One Language may be the best adapted, for Poetry and Eloquence, another for Philosophy and science, and another for Drollery and Humour. But that Language will be the best, which has most of these Characteristicks.

[1] The text of this entry is in JA's small, mature hand and appears on the last of the three pages he left blank in the midst of his undergraduate diary entries; see note on entry of 19 March 1754, above. The substance gives no clue to its date of composition, which has therefore been assigned to the period when most of the later entries in the Diary Fragment are known or believed to have been composed.

⟨9⟩ [WINTHROP'S LECTURES ON EXPERIMENTAL PHILOSOPHY.] APRIL 1ST. 1754.[1]

Mr. Winthrop began a series of Experimental Phylosophy,[2] and in the 1st place he explained to us the meaning, nature, and excellence of natural phylosophy, which is, (he says) the knowledge of those laws by which all the Bodys, in the universe are restrained, it being evident that not only those great masses of matter the heavenly Bodys, but all the minutest combinations of matter in each of them are regulated by the same general laws. For instance it is plain that all the planets observe exactly the same uniform rules in their revolutions round the sun, that every particle of matter observes on the surface of the earth.—As to the usefulness of natural phylosophy, to be convinced of that, it is necessary only to reflect on the state of all the Civilized nations of Europe, compared to many nations, in affrica, of as quick natural parts as Europeans, who live in a manner very little superiour to the Brutes.—The first Cause, and indeed the alpha and omega of natural phænomena, is motion, their being an utter impossibility that any effect should be produced in a natural way without motion, and ⟨this motion or rather Bodys in motion are subject to the following laws. 1st two bodys of different velocitys or swiftnesses, but æqual masses⟩ which motion is subject to Certain laws which he explained, and I have forgot. But thus much I remember, that motion, produced by gravity, was universally in right lines, from the body acted upon by gravity, to the Center of gravity, as the Center of the earth, for instance, or the like. He explained also, powers, weights, the line of direction of powers and weights, the Center of gravity, Center of ⊰ 10 ⊱ magnitude, and Center of motion, with the several methods of finding them, some of which I've forgot, and the rest he showed us examples of which cant easyly be exhibited. But by reason of some of these laws (he tells us) there are two famous towers in Italy, the one at Bolognia, and the other at [*Pisa*],[3] each near an hundred feet high which are not in a perpendicular position, but inclined to the horizon to a Certain degree, so as not to have the line of direction fall without the Base, because if the line of direction fell not within the Base, the buildings would inevitably fall. After this and many other things and Terms relating to motion, velocity &c. explained he dismiss'd us for the first time.—He touch'd also upon the advantages of gunpowder in war, above those of the Battering ram. For says he, the Battering ram was a hugh,[4] and unweildy peice of timber or rather combination of timbers, with an iron head much in the shape of a rams head, whence it drew its name, commonly weighing near forty thousand Pounds, and consequently required a 1000 men to manage it, a man being scarce able to handle more than 40 lb. with velocity enough to do execution. Now one of our cannon, by the almost irresistable force of rarifyed vapour will discharge a 36 pounder so as to make as large a Breach in a wall, as the Battering ram, and requires but ⟨*about 6*⟩ 5 or 6 men to order and direct it. Therefore 6 men can do as much execution now with a Cannon as 1000 could with a Battering ram, and the momenta are equal the velocity of the Cannon exceeding ⊰ 11 ⊱ that of the ram, as much as the ram exceeds the Cannon in weight, that is as 36:40000.

[1] This is the true beginning of JA's notes on Professor John Winthrop's lectures; he had first started them two pages earlier in the MS and then canceled that beginning for reasons explained in the note there (p. 55, above); see also note on entry of 19 March 1754, above.

All the notes on Winthrop, which continue through 11 April, are in JA's variant or experimental hand of 1754–early 1756, discussed in the Introduction.

[2] The "Course" or series of lectures on Experimental Philosophy was required by the terms of the Hollis profes-

sorship to be given at least once a year. Designated "private lectures," they were intended only for the sophisters (*Endowment Funds of Harvard University*, Cambridge, 1948, p. 55–56; Morison, *Three Centuries of Harvard*, p. 80). The terminal dates of a course of lectures such as this did not coincide with term times but rather with the period between March and the end of June when senior sophisters were required to be in Cambridge; see note on entry of 29 June 1753.

The notes taken by JA on the lectures indicate that the course as begun in 1754 was to be essentially the same as the thirty-three lectures prepared by Professor Winthrop for delivery one to five times a week (ordinarily three), from 10 March to 16 June 1746, a lecture-by-lecture summary of which in Winthrop's hand, with additions for 1747, is preserved in MH-Ar: "The Summary of a Course Of Experimental Philosophical Lectures, by Mr. J. Winthrop." A facsimile of Winthrop's outline of the first lecture is reproduced as an illustration in the present volume.

[3] Editorially supplied for a careless omission in MS. Winthrop's "Summary" does not mention the towers.

[4] Thus in MS.

APRIL 3D. 1754.

The second lecture, which was wholly taken up in explaining the Propertys of the Centers of gravity and motion, which were applyed to the instruments, Cheifly in use in Common life, such as, the lever, pulley, Ballance axis in peritrocheo,[1] &c. But the Ballance was principally insisted on. The reason of it was fully explained and the method of weighing, viz the distances of the Bodys from the Center of motion, must be precisely in a reciprocall proportion of their quantitys of matter or weights, always alowing for the weight of the Beam on which they are suspended, as well as friction, and the falsity of the supposition, that radii proceeding from the center of the earth are parrellel. Mr. Winthrop also demonstrated to us that all the advantages arising from any of the engines in use, resulted from the different possion [position] of them, with relation to force and velocity, thence he shew'd the famous problem of Archimedes viz, to move any weight however great by any force however small.—I had like to have forgot that he applied the doctrines of the center of gravity to the heavenly Bodys, shewing us the affections of the sun and planets with respect to their Centers of gravity, and instructed us in the manner of finding the Common Center of gravity of any 2 of 'em e.g. earth and moon, viz By this proportion as the quantitys of matter in Both added together is to the quantity of matter in the one separtely so is the distance of their centers to the distance of the Center of the other, from the Common Center sought. And to find the common Center of gravity of 3, 4 or 5 or any given number of Bodys, having found the common center of any 2, from that said Center draw a line to another of said Bodys and find the common Center of gravity of these two respecting the ⋇{ 12 }⋇ common Center of gravity of the former 2 as a Body containing a quantity of matter equal to Both said Bodys.

[1] See *OED* under Peritrochium, quoting John Harris, *Lexicon Technicum* (1704): "The use of this *Peritrochium* is to make the Cylinder or Axis be turned the more easily by the means of Staves or Levers, which are fix'd in its Circumference." See also Thomas Jefferson's Notes of a Tour through Holland and the Rhine Valley in 1788:

"A machine for drawing light *empty* boats over a dam at Amsterdam. It is an Axis in peritrochio fixed on the dam. From the dam each way is a sloping stage. The boat is presented to this, the rope of the axis made fast to it, and it is drawn up. The water [on one] side of the dam is about 4.f. higher than on the other" (Jefferson, *Papers*, ed. Boyd,

13:9).

Evidently Winthrop dealt in more detail with this mechanical device in a later lecture; see entry of 6 April, below.

APRIL 5TH. 1754.

The theory of the Ballance, scales, steel-yard &c. ⟨*and all*⟩ and the 3 species of lever's continued to which (viz) the lever he referred allmost all the instruments in life, and universally. To make a æquilibrium, the product of the quantity of matter in the weight multiplyed into its distance from the Center of motion, must be equal to the quantity of matter in the power, multiplyed into it's distance from said Center.

APRIL 6TH. 1754.

⟨*The phænomina of*⟩ The nature of the Pulley, axis in peritrochæo, and inclined Plane explained, which all depend on the laws before laid down (viz) that the quantity of matter in the weight bears the same proportion to the quantity of matter in the power, as the distance of the power from the Center of motion, to the distance of the weight from said Center.

APRIL 8TH. 1754.

The Theory of simple machines and in particular of the inclined plane, of the wedge and screw, and other machines compounded of these simple ones, finish'd.

APRIL 9 1754.

Sir Isaac Newtons three laws of nature proved and illustrated, together with the application of them to the planets, which are kept in their orbits by two forces acting upon them, viz that of gravity and that which is call'd their Centrifugal force whereby ⟨*it*⟩ they strives to recede from the Center of their orbits, and fly off therefrom in tangents.

⟨13⟩   APRIL 10, 1754.

The theory of Centrifugal forces, continued; and aplyed to the Cases of the planets; and from this Centrifugal force, Mr. Winthrop confuted the hypothesis of vortices, from this also arises the spheroidal form of the earth.

APRIL 11 1754.[1]

Some thing's observed concerning gravity, which encreases as you approach the Center of the earth in a reciprocal proportion of the squares of the distances, and under this head were introduced pendula and we saw that all pendula of equall length oscilated in equal time whether the arches they described were greater or less. We were also inform'd that bodys falling in Chords of a Circle will fall in equal times Cæteris paribus; and in the same time that the same Body would pass through the diameter, as

[1] JA's notes on Winthrop's course of lectures end with this entry, for the very good reason that Winthrop broke off his course this year with the eighth lecture in order to travel to Philadelphia, where he met his fellow scientist and correspondent Benjamin Franklin for the first time. His trip kept him away from Cambridge from 15 April to 24 May. See his MS Diary for 1754 (MH-Ar); also Sibley-Shipton, *Harvard Graduates*, 9:246–247.

The present entry also ends JA's efforts (so far as we know) to keep a diary as a Harvard student, although he was not graduated until July 1755. As explained in the Introduction, an interval of more than four years passed before he made further use of the folio MS designated as the Diary Fragment. When, in Oct. 1758, he did so—having already begun in Nov. 1755 a diary record in pocket form—he used the MS for different and very miscellaneous purposes rather than as, strictly speaking, a diary; see the following entries.

⟨14⟩ [LETTERS TO THREE FRIENDS ON STUDYING LAW, OCTOBER–NOVEMBER 1758.][1]

To [*John*] Wentworth.[2]

Mon Ami

My letters, for the future will come to you, not from a School House but from the Cell of an Hermit. I am removed from Worcester to Braintree where I live secluded from all the Cares and Fatigues of busy Life in a Chamber which no mortal Visits but myself except once in a day to make my Bed. A Chamber which is furnished in a very curious manner, with all sorts of Hermetical Utensils.

Here, no Idea of a Lady, of Diversions, of ⟨gay Life⟩ Business or of Pleasure ever enters. Here I read, smoke, think, and sleep. Old Roman Lawyers, and dutch Commentators are my constant Companions. What ample Provision have I here accumulated for lasting Felicity! The only Thing I fear is, that all my Passions, which you know are the Gales of Life, as Reason is the Pilot, will go down into an everlasting Calm. And what will a Pilot signify, if there is no Wind.

To prevent this I must intreat you to redouble your Letters, which

always raise a full Gale of Love, sometimes almost a Tempest of Emu-
lation and some times a Breeze of Envy, and will be sufficient, in
Addition to those of a few other Friends, to waft the Vessell, tho she
is not the best of sailors, with full Speed, along the Voyage.—But what,
and where is the Port of my Destination? In sincerity I am afraid to tell
you. Tis however a Harbour, where every Vessell may ride securely.
A Harbour, in which, tho Tempests rage around, and Thunders roll
above, and Earthquakes shudder beneath, neither the Vessell, her
Cargo or her Crew, ever receive any Damage.

But to be plain, I am beginning Life anew. I have new Friendships
to make, new Employments to follow, new Concerns, Prospects and
Studies, opening before me. And now I have mentioned Studies, I find
my self entering an unlimited Field. A Field in which Demosthenes,
Cicero, and others of immortal Fame have exulted before me! A Field
which incloses the whole Circle of Science and Literature, the History,
Wisdom, and Virtue of all ages.—Shall I dare to expatiate here in full
Career, like the nobler Animals, that range at large, or shall [I] blindly,
basely creep, like the mole, or the weezell?—Tell me.

To [*Tristram*] Dalton.[3]

How long is it my Friend, since I either received a Letter from you
or you from me? Some years I believe. And how long will it be, e'er
another Letter passes between us? Why If I may judge of the future
by the past, I shall receive one from you about 6 months hence, and
then an Intermission of 2 or 3 years will succeed. This has been the
Course of our Correspondence, and perhaps you would be as well
pleased, if the Intermission should be of 2 or 3 Centuries, or inper-
petuo instead of 2 or 3 years. You need not hope however to escape so.
Whenever I am fatigued with roman Lawyers and Dutch Commentators, I will set down, and ⟨*discharge the Vapours of the Brain, upon
Paper, and send it away to you*⟩ write to you, as Painters turn their
Eyes to a ⟨*green*⟩ mild pleasant Green Colour after long Attention to
black in order to ease and Relieve the Eye. This is said, (by the Way)
in Conformity to the common Place Cant of the present Day that The
study of Law is the most dry, unentertaining study in the World,
which I take to be full as wise as Lady ———s Contempt of Shakespears
Tragedies in the Lethe of Mr. Garrick.[4] You have heard many Persons
say that the study of Mathematicks and of Physicks is dry. Others can
find no Beauties in Poetry. And I believe them, as undoubtingly as I
believe some others, when they say that Law is dry. Every Thing, my
Friend, is dry in Proportion as it is not understood, and I shall not be

at all surprised to hear a young Spark whose ⟨*whole*⟩ Attention is dissipated among Horses and Ladies, (heaven forgive me) fiddles and frolicks, Cards and Romances, say that the Law is dry.

But to examine this Matter a little, can no Pleasure be found in tracing to their original sources in Morality, in the Constitution of human Nature, and the Connections and Relations of human Life, the Laws which the Wisdom of perhaps fifty Centuries, has established for the Government of human Kind. ⟨*No Pleasure in studying the Eloquence of Greece and Rome in those stupendous Monuments of it which have been the Wonder and Delight of every Age, to the present Day?*⟩ No Pleasure in the Study of those Remains, those precious Remains of grecian and roman Eloquence, which have been ⟨*the wonder and delight of*⟩ preserved to the Admiration of all Ages, down to the present day? ⟨*Far otherwise,*⟩ So far [otherwise?] that I assure you, even the ⟨*most*⟩ Common Law of England, and the precedents and [Statutes?] of former Times, which are most venomously [misused?] at this day, when once their [...] Language is understood, afford ⟨*us all*⟩ the Pleasure of Reasoning in as [great?] Perfection as your favourite science of Mathematicks ⟨*with the Exception only that we have not always that absolute Certainty, that we have in Mathematicks.*⟩[5]

⊰{ 15 }⊱ Tis true, we are not able to attain, in every Case of Law, that total Certainty which you have in some Problems and Theorems, nor have you in Mathematicks, the success in every Problem which you have in some.

To Samll. Quincy.[6]

⟨*How surprizingly we how inviolably*⟩

How resolutely, how inviolably, how surprizingly we have preserv'd and pursued The Resolution ⟨*we took*⟩ of writing each other upon ⟨*Law.*⟩ Points of Law, which we took at Weighmouth.—⟨*But*⟩ Oh my Friend how easily we are ⟨*bro't*⟩ fired to lawdable Determinations! But ⟨*oh*⟩ proh Dolor, how soon are such Determinations forgot?—Quite as suddenly as the Vows of perpetual Constancy made by a young Fellow, when in the most violent Hurry. This has some how or other recalled to my Memory a Pice of Advice, which Polonius gives to his Daughter in Shakespears Hamlet.

> I do know
> When the Blood burns, how prodigal the soul
> Lends the Tongue Vows. These Blazes oh my Daughter
> Giving more Light than Heat, extinct in both,
> You must not take for Fire.

The soul is no less Prodigal in lending the Tongue Vows, when the Blood glows with Ambition of getting Learning or Virtue, than when it burns with a very different Passion, the Passion alluded to in these Lines. And perhaps the Protestations of the Lover, are as sincere as the Resolutions of the scholar. And as the generous Lover, who by such Vows, has deceived and deflowered an innocent, virtuous Lady, would think him self bound in Honour, and in Conscience, to fullfill his Promises, so should the generous Schollar esteem it a violation of his Conscience, a base, ungenerous, debauching and ruining of himself, to forget his Vows of Industry.

For my own Part, my Conscience reproaches me with a long series of such Self Perfidy! I start sometimes, and shudder at myself, when the Thought comes into my mind how many million Hours I have squandered in a s[t]upid Inactivity neither furnishing my mind nor exercising my Body. Yet new Reflections continue to arise, and I every Day determine to begin a new Course of Life tomorrow. My Resolutions are like bubbles, they are perpetually rising to the surface of the stream and then are [broke?] and vanish by every puff of Wind. Yet new ones rise and die in perpetual succession.

In order to connect the preceeding Letter with this, let me add [that?] to taste this Pleasure, active Industry, and not now and then a sudden Resolution alone, is necessary.—And now I have mentioned Resolutions how [unwilling?] and [*remainder missing*] [7]

[1] The whole of this entry, like those that follow it, is in JA's small, mature hand. For the date assigned to this group of letter-drafts as a whole, see the Introduction, p. 10–11.

[2] John Wentworth (1737–1820), later Sir John, was a classmate, correspondent, and, until the Revolution separated them, a warm friend of JA's. He became the last royal governor of New Hampshire, a loyalist exile, and lieutenant governor of Nova Scotia.

Much of the correspondence between JA and Wentworth has been lost. In the *New England Historical and Genealogical Register*, 5 (1851):414/6, appears an undated letter from JA to Wentworth, which is known in no other version and which creates a small puzzle concerning the letter-draft in JA's Diary Fragment. The printed letter touches on the very topics dealt with in the draft (though in entirely different language),

was certainly sent because it was in the hands of a Wentworth descendant in 1851, and begins: "I resume with Pleasure my long neglected Pen ... to inform you that I am still alive, and well; that I am removed from Worcester to Braintree where I expect to live and die." It must therefore have been written in Oct. or Nov. 1758 and virtually precludes the possibility that the present letter, making the same announcement, was actually sent. Or was it sent to someone other than Wentworth, the stated addressee?

On Wentworth see JA, *Diary and Autobiography*, 1:4; 2:308; 4:85; Lawrence Shaw Mayo, *John Wentworth*, Cambridge, 1921; Sibley-Shipton, *Harvard Graduates*, 13:650–681.

[3] Tristram Dalton (1738–1817), of Newbury (later Newburyport), another classmate of JA's, "read law for pleasure" but married a rich wife and be-

came a merchant, shipowner, and U.S. senator (Sibley-Shipton, *Harvard Graduates*, 13:569–578; Benjamin W. Labaree, *Patriots and Partisans: The Merchants of Newburyport, 1764–1815*, Cambridge, 1964). The Adams Papers files show that Dalton and JA corresponded intermittently for over forty years.

⁴ *Lethe; or, Esop in the Shades*, a farce produced at Drury Lane in 1740 and afterward published, was David Garrick's first play. In it a character named Mrs. (not Lady) Riot tells Charon when she confronts him on the banks of the river Lethe: "Your Taste here, I suppose, rises no higher than your *Shakespears* and your *Johnsons*; oh you *Goats* and *Vandils!* in the Name of Barbarity take 'em to yourselves, we are tir'd of 'em upon Earth—one goes indeed to a Playhouse sometimes, because one does not know how else one can kill one's Time—every body goes, because—because—all the world's there."

⁵ In the MS of the Diary Fragment this is the point, between ⊰ 14 ⊱ and ⊰ 15 ⊱, where a leaf was slit out by JA,

leaving only a narrow stub. See the Introduction, p. 5.

⁶ Samuel Quincy (1734–1789), Harvard 1754, son of Col. Josiah Quincy of Braintree and brother of Hannah Quincy, the "Orlinda" of the Diary Fragment, studied law with Benjamin Prat and was admitted to the bar with JA in Nov. 1758. He and JA were to be friends, colleagues, and rivals until the Revolution, when Quincy, who held a lucrative crown office, took the loyalist side and became a permanent exile. See JA, *Diary and Autobiography*, 1:47, 50 ff., 109, 252; 2:2, 14, 72; 3:261, 273, 289, 295; *Adams Family Correspondence*, 1:122–123, 128, 130–131, 152; Sibley-Shipton, *Harvard Graduates*, 13:478–488. Copley's portrait of Quincy, about 1767, appears as an illustration in the present volume.

⁷ It is not beyond question whether this paragraph is part of the letter to Quincy or a detached reflection. But in respect to both substance and position (since it has a slight interval of space separating it from the preceding text) it appears to be distinct from the letter.

⊰ 15, *upside down* ⊱

[ON SOME FRIENDS WHO NOURISH WOUNDS IN THEIR HEARTS, OCTOBER–DECEMBER 1758.]¹

Vulnus alit Venis, et cæco carpitur igni.²

Alo, alere, alui, alitum, to nourish. Vulnus, a Wound or Hurt.

Carpo, carpere, carpsi, carptum, to waste away. Carpor to be [troubled?]. Carpitur, is consumed, wasted.

He nourishes a Wound in his Veins, and is consumed with a blind hidden fire.—Warner, Fessenden, Clark, Cranch, Quincy.³ All of them [cherished?] by their incessant Thinking, the Wound in their Hearts, and all consume, with a hidden internal flame.

¹ Nothing in this detached entry furnishes a clue to its date, but since it was inserted upside down in the blank space below the draft letter to Quincy, we may suppose that it was written after that draft was composed.

² Virgil, *Aeneid*, bk. IV, line 2. Said of Dido's secret passion for Aeneas.

³ Of the five persons listed, all of whom must have been Harvard, Worcester, or Braintree friends of JA's, two

bear names (Warner, Clark) too common to permit identification since they do not occur elsewhere in JA's early records. Fessenden is probably the "B[enjamin] Fessenden" with whom JA discussed Col. Josiah Quincy's character in April 1759 (JA, *Diary and Autobiography*, 1:81–82). Cranch is of course Richard Cranch, JA's most intimate friend, who had long nourished a "Wound" in his heart, inflicted by

Hannah Quincy. Writing from Worcester, 18 Oct. 1756, JA told Cranch that it would be a great triumph if he could "conquer a Passion for a Lady so greatly accomplished as Mrs. [i.e. Mistress, Miss] H—— Q. . . . [T]he more engaging the charms of her person and the more distinguished the Refinements of her Mind, the more noble your Resolution will appear" (Tr, Adams Papers, Microfilms,

Reel No. 114). That Cranch was still in Hannah's toils in 1758 seems evident from JA's letter to him about "Orlinda" in the following entry in the Diary Fragment. As for the last name in JA's list, it is no doubt that of Samuel Quincy, who was at this time courting Hannah Hill of Boston, whom he later married; see Sibley-Shipton, *Harvard Graduates*, 13:479–480.

{16} [A LETTER TO RICHARD CRANCH ABOUT ORLINDA,
A LETTER ON EMPLOYING ONE'S MIND, AND REFLECTIONS
ON PROCRASTINATION, GENIUS, MOVING THE PASSIONS,
CICERO AS ORATOR, MILTON'S STYLE, &C.,
OCTOBER–DECEMBER 1758.][1]

What is Wisdom? Is it, to write dramatic Poetry, like Milton or Shakespear? Is it to write on Astronomy and Physicks like Newton, or is it to know the human mind like Lock? Does it consist in Genius and Learning? No Genius and Learning have been oftener mad than wise. It is not to Act or think beyond man kind.

[Draft of a Letter to Richard Cranch.][2]

Say was there most of Cruelty or of Cunning in sealing up this cruel scroll ⟨this *Paper full of Disappointment, Spleen and Heart Ache*⟩ in a Letter from you.[3]—As the Doctor, to cheat his Patients Eyes, conceals his bitterest Potions in the sweetest Consalves[4] and Confections, as the Manchineal conceals her Poisonous Juices under the Appearance of a fair delicious Fruit,[5] as the Bee conceals her self and her fatal Sting in the Center of an Honey Comb, ⟨*in the same manner*⟩ Orlinda incloses this Paper, full of Disappointment, Spleen and Heart Ach, in a Letter from my dearest Friend!

You are sensible, my Friend, that the night Working Fancy of a Lover which steals him often, o'er seas and mountains to the ⟨*Arms*⟩ Company of his Mistress, and which figures, in his Slumbers, a thousand various scenes of Pleasure, only serves to increase his Misery, when he wakes, by ⟨*the Thought, that he cant possibly partake such Pleasures is too far* [removed?] *cannot possibly enjoy*⟩ exciting Desires which he cannot gratify. Just so this ⟨*Letter*⟩ Billet has roused in my Imagination a scene of Pleasure, which I should not otherwise have ⟨*wished for*⟩ tho't of,[6] a scene which seems to be grappled to my soul with Hooks of Steal, as immoveably as I wish to ⟨*be*⟩ grappled in ⟨*the*⟩ my Arms the Nimph, who gives it all its ornaments. ⟨*Wherever I go, whatever I do, asleep or awake, This dear bewitching scene attends me, and takes up all my Thoughts.*⟩ [7] If I look upon a Law Book and labor to exert all my Attention, my Eyes tis true are on the Book, but Imagination is at a Tea Table with Orlinda, seeing That Face, those Eyes, that Shape, that familiar friendly look, and [hear]ing Sense divine come mended from her Tongue. ⟨*When I should be at my Devotions*⟩ When the rest of the family are at their Devotions I am paying ⟨*mine*⟩ my Devoirs across a Tea Table to Orlinda. ⟨*When I attempt to Sle*⟩ I go to bed and lie ruminating on the same Ideas half the night, then fall asleep and dream about the same, till morning Wakes me, and robs me of my Bliss.[8] If, as grave folks say Madness is occasioned by too long and close an Attention to one set of Ideas, I shall soon I fear grow mad for I have had no Idea, but that of Orlinda, that Billet and Disappointment in my Head since you saw me.

Oh Tea, how shall I curse thy once delightful but now detested stream. May I never taste thy Waters more, for thy Waters will forever bring the Remembrance of Orlindas Cruelty, my eager Wishes and fatal Disappointment. Or if I must taste, for my Cup from thy stream may I drink whole Buckettsfull from Lethe to forget my Woe ⟨,*which that would otherwise without such an Antidote always renew*⟩.[9]

Shall such Cruelty go unpunished. No may she ⟨*have a husband*⟩ be in less than a year from this day be tied in the everlasting Chains of Wedlock.[10]

If he has the Spirit of a Man, he will be ready to bite his own Flesh.[11]

⟨ 17 ⟩ *[Draft of a Letter to an Unidentified Correspondent.]* [12]
My Friend

Such is the Nature of ⟨*Man*⟩ the human mind, that each individual must and will have some Employment, for his Thoughts, some ⟨*Amusement,*⟩ Business, study, Pleasure or Diversion, virtuous or vicious, lawdable or Contemptible, to consume his Time. If he is not instructed to contemplate the Heavens, he will instruct him self to contemplate Cockell shells and Pebblestones; if his Rank and Fortune exempt him from ⟨*Labour*⟩ Business, he will engage himself in Study or in Play, in Hunting or ⟨*whoring,*⟩ or something else, better or worse. The first Question, then that a young man should ask himself is, what Employment am I by the Constitution of my mind and Body, and by the Circumstances of Education, Rank and Fortune, directed to pursue? And the next is what is the best Method, the safest, easiest, nearest Road to the proper End of that Employment I have chose?

Suppose you had chosen the study of Nature, for the Business of your Life, should you not inquire in the first Place, what is the End of that study? Is it to improve the Manufactures, the Husbandry, or the Commerce of Mankind, or is it to adorn a Library with Butterflies of various sizes, Colours and shapes? Or suppose you had chosen the study of History, should you not inquire is the End of this study the naked Knowledge of great Names and [... Actions?] or is it a personal Improvement in Virtue and Capacity, by imitating the Virtues and avoiding the Vices of great men, and by judging of the Effects of Causes now at Work, by those Causes which have appeared heretofore? Should a Student in History inquire chiefly of the Dress, Entertainments and Diversions, instead of the Arts, Characters, Virtues and Opinions of ancient Nations, and the Effects of these on their public and private Happiness would not you laugh? There was nothing in the Lamp, by which Demosthenes wrote his orations, that deserved the Attention of the present Race of men, more than there is in the Candle by which I write this Letter. And I would pay no more Admiration to a man who could [tell] [13] me the exact Highth of Cicero, or the Number of Hairs that grew upon his Head, a Pice of Knowledge that I cannot now attain, than I would to one who could tell me the exact Number of Letters, Comma's and semicolons that are in all his Works, which [I] [14] have the means of knowing.

We are not therefore, to measure of Admiration of a man by the Number alone, but by the ⟨Importance, Usefulness and⟩ Utility and Number jointly of the Propositions that he knows, and his Dexterity in apply[ing] them to Practice.

⟨*The great secret therefore, the main*⟩ The primary Endeavour therefore, should be to distinguish between Useful and unuseful, to pursue the former with unwearied Industry, and to neglect with much Contempt all the Rest. We need not fear that subjects of Inquiry will be so few, that the Treasures of useful Knowledge will be exhausted.— Every Moment of the longest Life, may be spent in acquiring Knowledge of the greatest Moment, in the Course of Life.

Perhaps many hundreds, in the English Nation, have employed the same ⟨Attention,⟩ Industry, and Sagacity in discovering the Properties of Animalcules that Escape the natural sight, as Sir Isaac Newton did in discovering and demonstrating the true system of the World. I will venture yet further, perhaps these men, if they had employed Experiment and [Geometry?] in the [method?] he used would have made as wonderfull discoveries. It [is] [15] the Method then, and not the Drudgery of science that is chiefly to be [pursued? pressed?].

Why am I so silly as to trifle away my Time in such ⟨*useless*⟩ unprofitable scribbling—waste Paper, Pen, Ink, Time, Wood, Candles, in this idle Amuzement.

⫷ 18 ⫸ What is the Cause of Procrastination? To day my Stomack is disordered, and my Thoughts of Consequence, unsteady and confused. I cant study to day but will begin tomorrow. Tomorrow comes. Well, I feel pretty well, my head is pretty clear, but Company comes in. I cant yet study tomorrow, but will begin in earnest next day. Next day comes. We are out of Wood, I cant study: because I cant keep a fire. Thus, something is always wanting that is necessary.

What are the Proofs, the Characteristicks of Genius?—Answer Invention of ⟨*a System*⟩ new Systems or Combinations of old Ideas.
The Man, who has a faculty of inventing and combining into one Machine, or System, for the Execution of some Purpose and Accomplishment of some End, a great Number and Variety of Wheels, Levers, Pullies, Ropes &c. has a great Mechanical Genius. And the Proofs of his Genius, (unless it happen by mere luck) will be proportionably to the Number, and Variety of Movements, the Nice Connection of them, and the Efficacy of the entire Machine to answer its End. The last, I think at present, ought to be considered in [estimating?] any Genius. For altho Genius may be shewn in the Invention of a complicated Machine, which may be useless, or too expensive, for the End proposed, yet one of the most difficult Points is to contrive the Machine in such a manner, as to shorten, facilitate, and cheapen, any Manufacture &c. For to this End a Man will be obliged to revolve in his Mind perhaps an hundred Machines, which are possible but too unwieldy or expensive, and to select from all of them, one, which will answer the Purposes mentioned.
2. The Man who has a Faculty of feigning ⟨*a great Number, and Variety of Characters, Actions, Events &c.*⟩ and combining into one regular, correct, consistent Plan or Story, a great Number and Variety of Characters, Actions, Events &c. has a great poetical Genius. And the Proofs of his Genius are in Proportion to the Variety, Consistency and Number of his Characters, Actions and Events; and to the nice Connection and Dependence of these upon each other thro a whole Poem. And these Proofs have been given in a surprizing degree by

Milton and Shakespear, Homer, Virgil &c. Milton has feigned the Characters of Arch Angells and Devills, of Sin, Death, &c., out of his own creative Imagination and has adjusted, with great Sagacity, every Action and Event in his whole Poem to these Characters.

3. The Man, who has a Faculty of inventing Experiments and [reasoning?] on them [means?] of Starting new Experiments from that Reasoning, and on these Experiments forming new Reasonings till he reduces all his Experiments, all his Phenomena, to general Laws and Rules, and combines those Rules to an orderly [and re]gular Dependance on each other, thro the whole System, has a great Phylosophic Genius.

4. The Man who has a Faculty of considering all the faculties and Properties of human Nature, as the Senses, Passions, Reason, Imagination and faith, and of ⟨combining⟩ classing all these into order, into Rules, for the Conduct of private Life, has a great Genius in Morality.

5. He who has a Faculty of combining all these into Rules, for the Government of Society, to procure Peace, Plenty, Liberty, has a great political Genius.

Thus Order, Method, System, Connection, Plan, or whatever you call it, is the greatest Proof of Genius, next to Invention of new Wheels, Characters, Experiments, Rules, Laws, which is perhaps the first and greatest. Q[uery]. Does not the Word Invention express both these faculties, of inventing Wheels &c. and putting them in order.

Q. May not Genius be shewn in aranging a Mans Diet, Exercise, Sleep, Reading, Reflection, Writing &c. in the best order and Proportion, for His Improvement in Knowledge?

These are but vague, general, indeterminate Reflections. I have not Patience to pursue every particular attentively. But, This Patience ⟨is the greatest Attainment⟩ or a great Superiority to a mans own unsteadiness, is perhaps one of the greatest Marks of Genius. Inatention, Wandering, Unconnected Thoughts, are the opposites to this Patience.

Q[uery]. Had not Mr. [Prat?] some such Reflections in his mind, when he said that Mr. Edwards had given proofs of a Great Genius.[16] —And Q. is not The Pilgrims Progress, according to these Rules, a Proof of a great Genius.—There is Invention.[17]

⟨19⟩ Ballast is what I want, I totter, with every Breeze. My motions are unsteady.

Of what use to a Lawyer is that Part of oratory, which relates to the moving of the Passions? Without Simplicity no human Performance can arrive to any great Perfection.

The Talent, and Art of moving the Passions, may be used in a Capital Trial by the Counsel for the King, to raise the Resentment of the Jury, against the Crimes of the Prisoner, and by the Counsell for the Prisoner, to move the Compassion of the Jury.

It may be used to raise, in the Judges, Jury and Spectators, an Admiration, and Esteem of the wise, humane, equitable and free Constitution of Government we are under. It may be used to rouse in the Breasts of the Audience a gallant Spirit of Liberty, especially when declaiming upon any Occasion, on any Instance of arbitrary Conduct in an Officer or Magistrate.

Sound is I apprehend a more powerful Instrument of moving the Passions than Sense. Musick is capable of raising in the Mind every tender, generous, noble Passion and Sentiment. And as a Musician, to get the skill of moving the Passions, must study the Connection between sounds and Passions, so should an orator. Every Passion has its distinct peculiar sound. Anger, and Compassion, produce very different Modulations of the Voice, and so do fear, Love, Contempt, Joy, sorrow, and Admiration. An Orator to gain the Art of moving the Passions, must attend to Nature, must observe the Sounds in which all sorts of People, express the Passions and sentiments of their Hearts, and must learn to adapt his own Voice, to the Passion he would move. The easiest Way to this will be to possess his own Mind strongly, with the Passion he would raise, and then his Voice will conform it self of Course. Thus if you will raise in a Jury a Resentment of some great Crime, resent it strongly yourself, and then the boldest ⟨Expressions⟩ Thoughts and Words will occur to your mind, and utter themselves with the most natural Tone of Voice, Expression of Countenance and Gesture of your Body.

[Let] me examine in the greatest orators of Rome and Britain, what peculiar Sounds are used [to] express the different Emotions of the Mind—as Grief, Resentment, Fear, Horror, Courage, [Com]passion, Love, Joy &c. To examine this Point thoroughly would require a search [of] all the Poets and orators of all the Languages I understand.

Grief and Fear, in Tullies Oration for Milo,[18] are uttered by Interrogations, and Exclamations. Quid me reducem esse voluistis? An ut, inspectante me, expellerentur ei, per quos essem restitutus? Nolite

74

obsecro vos, pati mihi acerbiorem Reditum esse, quam fuerit ille ipse Discessus. Nam qui possum putare me restitutum esse, si distrahar ab iis, per quos restitutus sum? Utinam dii immortales fecisse[n]t (pace tua, Patria, dixerim).¹⁹ This Figure which addresses Things without Life, as a Country, a Temple, a Monument, Virtue or Vice, Wisdom, Folly &c. as if they were Personages, is much used both in Poetry and oratory. [...] says,

> Welcome for thee fair Virtue all the Past.
> For thee fair Virtue welcome even the last.

He looks and speaks to Virtue as Tully looks and speaks to Patria his Country.—I believe tis called Apostrophe some times. Popes Address to L.B. in the Conclusion of his Ethic Epistles, is called an Apostrophe. [C]ome then my friend my Genius come along, Oh Master of the Poet and the Song.²⁰

The Point, that Tully drives at, is the Acquittal of Milo. He is afraid that the Judges will sentence him to death or Banishment. It is Lachrimis non movetur Milo &c.²¹ His design here is to raise their Admiration of Miloes strength and Constancy of mind and of his Love of Virtue and Contempt of Exile. Then he speaks, in pungent, keen Questions, to the Judges. Vos Iudices quo tandem animo Eritis? Memoriam Milonis retinebitis, ipsum ejicietis? Et erit dignior Locus in Terris ullus, qui hanc Virtutem excipiat quam hic qui procreavit?— Thus I see that any great Agitation of mind breaks out into exclamations and Interrogations.—Vos, Vos appello fortissimi Viri. There is great Warm[th] in that Repetition of Vos, qui multum pro Republica sanguinem effudistis Vos in viri et in civis invicti appello periculo, Centuriones, vos que militus; vobis non modo inspectantibus, sed etiam armatis, et huic Iudicio præsidentibus, hæc tanta Virtus ex hac Urbe expellatur? exterminabitur? projicietur? ⟨*An Address with so much Vehemence*⟩ An Appeal to the Centurions and soldiers, complimenting them with the Epithet fortissimi Viri made with so solemn and vehement a Repetition Vos Vos, and feeling with so much sensibility, the Ingratitude, Cruelty, and folly of Banishing a Man who had rendered the Republic such Important services and was able and zealous to render still more, must have drawn Tears to their Eyes and Rage to their Breasts. His Mind seems to waver between Indignation at Clodius, and Admiration of Milo, between Love and Gratitude to Milo for his past favours to him and Services to the State, and Fear, dread of his Banishment. His Mind is a Ship in a Tempest, tossed and tumbled

75

with great Impetuosity, every Way. He breaks out into Exclamations to the Immortal Gods, and to the happy Coasts that shall receive Milo when banished and to his own ungrateful miserable Country if she shall banish him. I take it this Peroration for Milo, may be studied as a Model of the Pathetic.

I should distinguish between moving the Passions of another, as an Orator, and expressing Passion naturally, like a Dramatic Poet, for tho there may be an Affinity between them, yet they are distinct. Tully, in that Peroration, expresses the Passions of his own Mind, his Love, his Gratitude, his Grief and fear, and at the same time moves the Passions of the Judges, the Centurions and soldiers by appealing to them, to Heaven by exclaiming to his Country and that Country that should receive Milo if Banished, but a Dramatic Poet has to make each Character express his own Passions well, in order to raise the Passions of the Audience &c.

⟨20⟩ With what pathos does Othello bid farewell to War, in Shakespear.

> Oh now forever
> Farewell the tranquil Mind! farewell content;
> Farewell the ploomed Troops and the big War
> That make Ambition Virtue! Oh! farewell!
> Farewell the neighing Steed, and the shrill Trump
> The spirit stirring Drum, th'ear piercing fife
> The Royal Banner and all Quality,
> Pride, Pomp, and Circumstance of glorious War
> And Oh! you mortal Engines, whose rude Throats
> Th'immortal Joves dread Clamours counterfeit
> Farewell! Othello's Occupations gone! [22]

These Exclamations, Apostrophe's, express, with the utmost grandeur of sounds, the deep Grief, Misery, and despair that ⟨were in⟩ raged within his Mind. Q[uery], is Grief always so sonorous [23] and harmonious? Is it ever expressed in short broken sounds? I believe not, it always swells into numbers. I may say that Passion swells into Numbers, and Metaphors.

I have so many Irons in the Fire, that every one burns.—I have common, civil, natural Law, Poetry, Oratory, in Greek, latin, french, english to study, so that when I set down to read or think, so many subjects rush into my mind that I know not which to chuse.

But to what End this subtle Inquiry into Niceties.—A minute Examination of syllables and sounds will never procure Genius. But Genius has often hit without design upon the most grand and proper sounds.

What are the Motives, that ought to urge me to hard study? The Desire of Fame, Fortune and personal Pleasure. A critical Knowledge of the Greek and Roman ⟨*Tongues and of the*⟩ and french Poetry, History and Oratory, a thorough comprehensive Knowledge of natural, civil, common, and Province Law, will draw upon me the Esteem and perhaps Admiration, (tho possibly the Envy too) of the Judges of both Courts, of the Lawyers and of Juries, who will spread my Fame thro the Province, will draw around m[e a S]warm of Clients who will furnish me with a plentiful Provision for my own Support, and for the Increase of my fortune. And by means of this Authority and Consideration, with the Judges, Lawyers, Juries and Clients, I shall be able to defend Innocence, to punish Guilt, and to promote Truth and Justice among Mankind.—But besides these Motives, there is another, no less powerful than either, which is the active Acquisition of Knowledge, in a peaceful, undisturbed Retirement. Here I should moderate my Passions, regulate my Desires, increase my Veneration of Virtue, and Resolution to pursue it, here I should range the whole material and Intellectual World, as far as human Powers can comprehend it, in silent Contemplation.—Now, if Fame, Fortune, Pleasure and Virtue have not Power to influence me, what am I? ⟨*Oh Genius*⟩ Oh [...]![24] Oh Learning! Oh Eloquence! ⟨*how shall I*⟩ may I dare to think I have the first? How shall I assume a Power to command the other two. Knowledge I can and will acquire, and has Language Power to charm, and shall not I avail my self of that Power?

Longinus says there is an Art of the Sublime. Swift says there is an Art of the Profound. Q[uery]. What Rules will help us to acquire both or either. As the sublime is a Property of Discourse, whether in Speaking or Writing, some real Cause which produces in the Hearer or Reader, Transport and Rapture, no doubt, that Property may be found out by examining critically those Passages which produce that Effect, and by comparing them with other Passages which produce no such Effect, or a contrary Effect, as Drowsiness, &c. And when the true, real Cause is known, we may endeavour to infuse it into our Discourse —e.g. If this Cause consists in sound only, we must inquire what sounds have and what have not this Effect upon us. And we must

77

chuse out such Words, as have that sound and avoid others. If it consists in sounds, we must inquire whether it consists in the sound of a particular Word or in the combination of all the Words in a Period. If it consist in the Idea only, we should inquire what Ideas have this Effect on the human mind? And we shall find, that the Ideas of Objects that are great in Nature, as that of the Sun, Moon, the Sky, Earthquakes, Thunder, Tempests, Comets, extensive Prospects &c. have this Effect on the mind. If it consist in the sentiment, we must inquire what sentiments have this Effect on the Mind? And we shall find that fixed Resolutions in favour of Virtue, Courage, disinterested Charity, Generosity, Contempt of littlenesses &c. have this Effect.— Now from such observations as these, no doubt, Rules may be collected, and reduced into an Art for acquiring the sublime, the grand and noble, and for avoiding the low, little and mean in Discourse. I have not Leisure nor Patience, for examining the sublime Passages in Tully, Virgill, Milton, Shakespeare, Pope, Bolinbroke, Swift, Addison, Tillotson, Ovid, Horace &c. by these Rules. In that very sublime Passage in Milton where the Effect of Satans Speech upon his infernal Host is described,[25] The sublimity consists, Partly, in the sound of the Words, partly in the Ideas, that they convey, and partly in the Sentiments.—Out flew Millions of flaming Swords drawn from the [Thigh]s of Mighty Cherubim, the sudden Blaze far round illumind Hell, highly they ragd [Again]st the highest, ⟨and fierce⟩—Many of these Words, as flew, flaming, [...][26] drawn, mighty, Blaze, far, round, highly, ragd, have when pronounced seperately, a grand Sound, and here they are arranged into a very harmonious order.

⟨21⟩ And fierce with grasped Arms, clashd on the sounding Shields the Din of War, Hurling Defiance towards the Vault of Heaven.

The Words fierce, grasped, Arms, clashd, sounding, War have a loud grand sound and are so disposed in this Line, as both to elevate and quicken the Voice of the Reader, which makes the whole frame of both Reader and Hearer thril with Transport.

Then in the next Line, hurling, Defiance, Vault, have all a bold elevated sound.

Thus it seems that the bare sound of the Words, as disposed in this Passage, have an Effect upon the Hearer like the sound of a musical Instrument, playing some grand and sublime Tune.

Now let us examine the Ideas conveyed by these Sounds. Out flew— The Idea of Millions, a great, a surprizing Number of blazing swords. There is something great and terrible in the Idea of a single blazing glittering sword, because we associate with it, the Idea of Slaughter and Blood and Death, which naturally shock and arouse us, but when the Idea of Millions of blazing swords, as much larger than our swords as a Devil is supposed larger than a Man, flying instantaneously out from the scabbards of a whole Host of Devils, and brandished in air, enters the Mind it alarms, rouses, astonishes it. But then the sudden Blaze [created?] by all these Swords illumins all Hell. The Idea of a Flash of Lightning, is grand and elevating to the Mind, but a flash like this, that brightens the dark Abodes below, astonishes every mind. Then the Idea of grasping suddenly their Arms, Spears, Swords &c. and each one clashing his upon his shield, raises an Idea of a direful Clash, that neither Thunder, Earthquake nor Tempest, tho' all of them grand sounds can equall. Then the Din of War calls up the Ideas of all those sounds that attend an Army, the sound of Drums, Trumpetts, and all sorts of musical Instruments, the murmuring, shoutings, screamings of living and [dying?], which is very terrible and shocking to the Mind. Then come the Ideas of Hurling, which denotes strength and Activity, both of which are [...] and elevating, then of Defiance, which denotes a grand Temper of mind, then the Idea of the Vault of [Hea]ven, which is one of the sublimes[t] Objects in Nature.—It is scarce possi[ble to] conceive how a greater Number of great Ideas could be asserted [in] so few Lines.

[Lastl]y let us examine the Sentiments. The general sentiment is that of Rebellion and Warfare, proclaimed by all the infernal Host against the Almighty, which is a sentiment that cant fail to excite Horror and Astonishment in every human mind. Then comes a sentiment, that they raged against God which raises the [...] still higher, till at last it breaks out into open impious Defiance, scorn and Contempt, which compleats the Passage and makes the Blood of [every?] Reader, who has a soul, curdle from his fingers to his Toes.

Perhaps few Passages can be quoted, in any Language in Prose or Verse, where sounds, Ideas, and Thoughts [conspire? conform?] so perfectly and seem to [contend?] which shall produce most Astonishment in the Reader, with this.

N.B. Tho I always admired this Passage, and have repeated it 1000 times, yet I never found 1/2 so many Beauties in it as this Examination has laid open to my sight.

Thus we see in this Passage, not only soft and smo[o]th sounds but such as are harsh and grating, not only Ideas of Objects that are beautiful and lovely, but of such as are deformed and detestible, not only sentiments that are generous, grateful, noble, but such as are ungrateful, impious, horrible, may be employed in producing the sublime.

But to return. I collect from this Heap, that The Art of the sublime, like the Art of natural Philosophy is [formed? founded?] in a science, and that Experiment and Observation are the natural means of improving both. We must make Trial of the Effects of different Sounds, of different Ideas, and of different Sentiments, on the human Senses, Passions, Imagination, and Understanding, to discover general Rules for producing the Sublime and avoiding the low.

Tis desirable to know the general system of humanity, to know the most remarkable Things in this World.

[1] This very miscellaneous entry, occupying pages { 16–21 } of the MS as it survives, is actually a series of detached jottings, letter drafts, literary exercises, notes on books read, &c., which seem from the handwriting and the appearance of the MS to have been put down at the same period, although not all at once and not necessarily consecutively. That they all belong to the last three months of 1758 seems clear from the evidence adduced and discussed in the Introduction.

[2] The recipient's copy of this letter, bearing the addressee's name on the cover, is in the Adams Papers, having been returned at some point by a Cranch descendant. It is without date or signature (but see the discussion of its probable date, Nov.–Dec. 1758, in the Introduction, p. 13) and varies sufficiently from the draft to show that JA worked hard over his epistolary style; see the textual notes below.

On Richard Cranch (1726–1811), see Adams Genealogy; indexes to JA, *Diary and Autobiography* and to *Adams Family Correspondence*; Sibley-Shipton, *Harvard Graduates*, 11:370–376.

[3] That is to say, Cranch's letter (not found), to which JA is replying, enclosed a note (also not found) from "Orlinda." From what follows it would appear that Cranch and Hannah wrote their notes to JA during a gay rendezvous over a tea table. JA may have been invited, but he could not or at any rate did not attend. On the identification of "Orlinda" as Hannah Quincy, and JA's love affair with her, see the Introduction, p. 11–13.

[4] Thus also in RC. This spelling is not recorded, but the word is probably JA's fancy equivalent of "conserves."

[5] Manchineel: "A West Indian tree . . . having a poisonous and caustic milky sap, and acrid fruit somewhat resembling an apple" (*OED*).

[6] RC: "which my Pen cannot describe."

[7] RC adds a sentence at this point: "The Idea of this has engrossed my whole Attention."

[8] In RC this sentence reads: "I go to bed, and ruminate half the night, then fall asleep and dream of the same enchanting scenes till morning comes and brings Chagrin, fretfulness and Rage, in exchange for Bliss and Rest."

[9] It should be pointed out that it was over a tea table at Col. Quincy's that JA and Hannah Quincy had their first recorded, and very intimate and revealing, conversation, apparently early in Jan. 1759 (JA, *Diary and Autobiography*, 1:66–67).

[10] This wish, or curse, was almost literally realized. In the minds of Braintree people, even if not formally, Hannah Quincy and Dr. Bela Lincoln (1734–1773), of Hingham, her brother Sam's Harvard classmate, were engaged from at least early 1759—at the very time JA was nearly trapped into making a marriage proposal to her. The courtship did not go at all smoothly, but the marriage took place on 1 May 1760. See JA, *Diary and Autobiography*, 1:87–88, 102, 114, 118–119, 176–177; and, on Lincoln generally, Sibley-Shipton, *Harvard Graduates*, 13:455–457. A few months later JA described in shockingly vivid terms a scene between the new husband and wife that drove from his mind any bad wishes he had ever made for Hannah. In her own father's house

Lincoln "treated his Wife, as no drunken Cobler, or Clothier would have done, before Company. Her father never gave such Looks and Answers to one of his slaves." Examples follow of Lincoln's "hoggish" and "brutally rustic" conduct toward Hannah that made her sink "into silence and shame and Grief" (JA, *Diary and Autobiography,* 1:176-177).

Two things may be said of this account. JA's affection for "Orlinda" was not yet dead, and Hannah's fate was a sad one for a girl who had recently had many of the young men of Braintree at her feet. As things turned out, Bela Lincoln died before he was forty, and in 1777 his widow married a well-to-do Boston widower, Ebenezer Storer, merchant, deacon of the Brattle Square Church, and recently appointed treasurer of Harvard College—"an exceeding good match," as AA reported to her husband, "and much approved of" (*Adams Family Correspondence,* 2:356). Storer was famous for his kindness and good works, and the marriage was a long and happy one. (On Storer generally, see Sibley-Shipton, *Harvard Graduates,* 12:208-214.) The Adams Papers files show that AA sent Mrs. Storer news and patterns from Europe, and the families remained on cordial relations for many years.

Mrs. Storer long outlived her husband, as JA outlived AA. The history of JA's relationship with the fascinating Orlinda closes with an incident as dramatic as it is fitting. It was told by a great-nephew of Mrs. Storer, Josiah Quincy (1802-1882), author of a charming book of reminiscences. From boyhood he remembered a certain "sylvan spot," in that part of Braintree that became Quincy, which was always known as "Cupid's Grove" and plays a part in his anecdote. Sometime in the early 1820's young Quincy was "deputed to attend [his] venerable relative on a visit to the equally venerable ex-President," the Adams and the Quincy homesteads not being far apart.

"Both parties [Quincy relates] were verging upon their ninetieth year.... When Mrs. Storer entered the room, the old gentleman's face lighted up, as he exclaimed, with ardor, 'What! Madam, shall we not go walk in Cupid's Grove to-

gether?' To say the truth, the lady seemed somewhat embarrassed by this utterly unlooked-for salutation. It seemed to hurry her back through the past with such rapidity as fairly to take away her breath. But self-possession came at last, and with it a suspicion of girlish archness, as she replied, 'Ah, sir, it would not be the first time that we have walked there!' " (*Figures of the Past,* p. 56-57.)

[11] There is nothing to indicate to whom this passage, possibly a quotation, was meant to apply.

[12] The impersonal style and the general substance of the letter that follows suggest that it was written as a literary exercise rather than addressed to a friend. Possibly it was intended for newspaper publication.

[13] Editorially supplied.

[14] Editorially supplied.

[15] Editorially supplied.

[16] Apparently an allusion to remarks made by Benjamin Prat (1711-1763), Harvard 1737, a leader of the Boston bar and later chief justice of New York Province, in reference to the celebrated theologian and author Jonathan Edwards (1703-1758), Yale 1720. On Prat see Sibley-Shipton, *Harvard Graduates,* 10:226-239; on Edwards, *DAB.*

[17] It is at this point in the MS, between { 18 } and { 19 }, that three leaves (six pages) were slit out by JA for some other use, probably (but not certainly) before the present reflections were entered in the Diary Fragment. See the Introduction, p. 5.

[18] Relevant to the following analysis of Cicero's rhetoric and its actually physical effect on JA is the following passage, written at approximately the same time: "Thursday [21 Dec. 1758]. Yesterday and to day I have read loud, Tullius 4 Orations against Cataline. The Sweetness and Grandeur of his sounds, and the Harmony of his Numbers give Pleasure enough to reward the Reading if one understood none of his meaning. Besides I find it, a noble Exercise. It exercises my Lungs, raises my Spirits, opens my Porr[s], quickens the Circulations, and so contributes much to Health" (JA, *Diary and Autobiography,* 1:63).

[19] From Cicero's Speech on Behalf of Titus Annius Milo, §§37-38.

[20] These lines, addressed by Pope (as

JA says) to "L[ord] B[olingbroke]," are not from the "Ethic Epistles" or *Moral Essays*, but from the *Essay on Man*, Epistle IV, lines 373–374.

[21] This and the following quoted and paraphrased matter are from Cicero's Oration for Milo, §37.

[22] *Othello*, Act III, scene ii, lines 347–357.

[23] MS apparently reads "sonorerous."

[24] Here is an unresolved crux in the text, and, unfortunately, in a passage very revealing of JA's hopes and fears concerning himself—a passage, too, of some interest for the historian of ideas because of its distinction between "genius" in its then very newest sense and acquired knowledge and skills.

JA clearly first wrote: "Oh Genius! Oh Learning! Oh Eloquence!" and, hardly daring to ask himself if he had "the first" of these, he could comfort himself only with the realization that, with effort, he could acquire the other two—"Learning" (or "Knowledge") and "Eloquence" (or "Language [with] the Power to charm"). In shaping these thoughts he at some point crossed out the first of the three qualities in his list ("Genius"), but what he cramped into the space above it is utterly cryptic; perhaps "Gens" or Gius"—a hasty and contracted restoration of what he had originally written and then (wrongly) crossed out. Whatever he finally wrote, it seems unquestionable that he *meant* "Genius."

[25] *Paradise Lost*, bk. I, lines 663–669, whence the quoted and paraphrased matter below is taken.

[26] Corner of page torn away in MS.

EDITORIAL NOTE ON
THE CASE OF FIELD *v.* LAMBERT

By L. Kinvin Wroth and Hiller B. Zobel

A number of the later entries in the newly discovered Diary Fragment add precious scraps of information to the relatively little known of the very beginnings of John Adams' career as a lawyer. Much the most important among them are the notes and drafts, scattered and disorderly but substantial, that Adams prepared for his first case, Field *v.* Lambert. In combination with several entries in the *Diary* as published in 1961, these materials permit a detailed examination of this crucial and traumatic episode.[1]

The new materials on Field *v.* Lambert appear in three separate entries in the MS of the Fragment. In keeping with the editorial policy throughout this volume, they are printed in their original order at pages 89–90, 93–94, and 94–96, below. Within these entries five separate items may be distinguished. In the first entry are a brief discussion of the calling and name of mason and a list of queries concerning the declaration in the case. The second entry is a draft of the declaration. The third entry contains an alternative or revised passage from the declaration and some further notes and queries on it.

[1] JA's early career is summarized and pertinent references to his *Diary and Autobiography* are collected in JA, *Legal Papers*, 1:lv–lvii. The brief account of Field *v.* Lambert and the statement that JA's first action in the Suffolk Inferior Court was entered in July 1759 are inaccurate, as the present discussion demonstrates.

Editorial Note on Field v. Lambert

The case arose on 10 October 1758, when two of Luke Lambert's horses broke into Joseph Field's Braintree meadow "and lay there some time, damage feasant." When Lambert discovered the horses, he entered the meadow himself, anxious to avoid paying for any harm that they had done. Despite Field's active protests, Lambert "waved his Hat, and Screamed at" the horses, driving them away, "with[out] tendering Feild his Damages." Field, who had been unable to collect damages in an earlier similar incident, now brought suit against Lambert by making complaint before Justice Josiah Quincy, Adams' Braintree friend and neighbor. The defendant apparently did not appear when summoned, because Field obtained a warrant of contempt, "directed to the Constable, who brought the Offender before the Justice, attended with the Complainant, and the Witnesses ordered to be summoned." Adams was present at the hearing on the warrant, held on 13 October.[2] He was apparently not of counsel in the case, but sat in as friend, not only of the court, but of the only attorney who seems to have appeared, and presumably of the parties as well.

The legal gist of Field's case was that Lambert was guilty of a "Rescous," or rescue, an unlawful taking of property from one who is lawfully detaining it. Field's position was that he had been in the process of driving the offending animals to the town pound, where by law they could be boarded at the owner's expense.[3] His claim was based on a Province statute which provided that a person rescuing from one "about to drive them to the pound" animals which had been "taken up" after being "found damage-feasant in any . . . inclosure" should forfeit the sum of 40s. to the poor of the town and be liable for "all just damages" suffered by the rescuee.[4]

Justice Quincy never reached the merits of the case. Before he could proceed, his son Samuel, Adams' contemporary at the bar, "took Exception on the Warrant" in Lambert's behalf. In effect young Quincy was saying that his client could not be held in contempt, because the Justice had lacked jurisdiction in the original suit. The grounds of the exception were, first, that the total sum claimed in the suit (40s. forfeiture and 9s. damages) exceeded the statutory limit of 40s. placed on the jurisdiction of a single justice,[5] and, second, that an action under the statute could

[2] JA, *Diary and Autobiography*, 1:48 (13 Oct. 1758). For the earlier controversy between the two, see same, p. 50. This proceeding was apparently one under the Act of 18 June 1697, c. 8, §1, 1 Mass., *Province Laws* 282–283, providing that upon complaint of any "debt, trespass or other matter" within his jurisdiction, a justice of the peace was to grant a writ against the party complained of, to be served by the sheriff or other officer in the normal manner. "And in case of non-appearance upon summons duely served, being so returned by the officer, such justice may issue out a warrant of con-tempt, directed to the sheriff, or marshal, or other officer, as aforesaid, to bring the contemner before him, as well to answer the said contempt as the plaintiff's action." See also the form of a warrant for contempt, Act of 5 June 1701, c. 4, §1, same, p. 463.

[3] Act of 10 June 1698, c. 6, §§2, 3, same, p. 322–323.

[4] Act of 10 June 1698, c. 6, §4, same, p. 323, set out at p. 93, note 2, below.

[5] By Act of 18 June 1697, c. 8, §1, same, p. 282, "all manner of debts, tres-passes and other matters, not exceeding the value of forty shillings (wherein the title of land is not concerned), shall

83

be brought only in a "court of record" and that the court of a single justice was not such a court. Justice Quincy forthwith ordered an adjournment that he might "inform himself" upon the two points raised.[6]

In his Diary, following his account of the proceeding, Adams noted several questions involved in the court-of-record problem.[7] These notes support his subsequent assertion that he had been the first to suggest the lack of jurisdiction. Nearly a month later Justice Quincy reported that he had learned from a fellow justice of the peace that his was indeed not a court of record. Quincy boasted of the acumen of his son "Sammy," who "was all along of that Opinion," but affected not to remember Adams' position on the question. Adams squirmed under the slight, asking himself, "Was forgetfulness, was Partiality, or was a cunning Design to try if I was not vain of being the Starter of the Doubt [as to jurisdiction], the true Cause of" it?[8] No record has been found, but the Diary entries indicate that, whoever raised them, these jurisdictional issues were the basis for a dismissal of Field's action.

Thereafter, Adams was retained by Field to bring a new action against Lambert. On 18 December he delivered to his client "a Declaration in Trespass for a Rescue," about which he expressed manifold misgivings:

I was obliged to finish it, without sufficient examination. If it should escape an Abatement, it is quite indigested, and unclerklike. I am ashamed of it, and concerned for it. If my first Writt should be abated, if I should throw a large Bill of Costs on my first Client, my Character and Business will suffer greatly. It will be said, I dont understand my Business. No one will trust his Interest in my hands. I never Saw a Writt, on that Law of the Province. I was perplexed, and am very anxious about it. . . . How this first Undertaking will terminate, I know not. I hope the Dispute will be settled between them, or submitted, and so my Writt never come to an Examination.[9]

It is Adams' draft of this declaration, seeking 40s. forfeiture and 20s. damages, which appears in the Diary Fragment in the second of the entries that relate to Field *v.* Lambert.

The court in which Adams intended to enter the action cannot be determined with certainty on the basis of present evidence. The most likely possibilities are (1) that it was to be a suit in the Suffolk County Inferior Court of Common Pleas and (2) that it was simply to be a new proceeding before Justice Quincy or another local justice of the peace.[10]

---

and may be heard, tryed, adjudged and determined, by any of his majestie's justices of the peace within this province, in their respective precincts."

[6] JA, *Diary and Autobiography*, 1:48–49.

[7] Same, p. 49–50.

[8] Same, p. 57–58 (5? Nov. 1758).

[9] Same, p. 62–63 (18 Dec. 1758).

[10] Although it is possible that the action was to have been brought in the Bristol or Plymouth County Inferior Courts, which also had December terms (Act of 23 April 1743, c. 32 §1, 3 Mass., *Province Laws* 64), this seems improbable, because a writ served on 18 December would have been too late for either court under the statutory rule that service must be had at least fourteen days prior to the sitting of the court at which the writ was returnable. Act of 26 June 1699, c. 2, §3, 1 Mass., *Prov-*

If Field's first action before Quincy was in fact disposed of upon jurisdictional grounds, it seems unlikely that Adams would have proceeded again before a justice of the peace. There is other evidence that the second action was in the Suffolk Inferior Court. The fact that the declaration sought damages in the lump sum of £3 suggests that Adams was not overly concerned with monetary limits on jurisdiction. Moreover, 18 December was the day before the deadline for the service of writs to be returned to the January 1759 Suffolk Inferior Court, which sat on 2 January.[11] This fact might explain the necessity for hasty drafting which Adams lamented in the Diary entry just quoted. The importance which Adams attached to the matter in that Diary entry also suggests that he was about to walk upon a stage broader than that of a justice's court. That he did at least some business at the January Inferior Court, appears from his writ in Adams *v.* Penniman, dated 19 December, which was entered at that term.[12] Finally, in his later queries about the writ, appended to the first Field *v.* Lambert entry in the Diary Fragment, Adams spoke of the alternative possibility of filing "an Information . . . vs. Lambert this Court," which could well have meant at the then current term of the Inferior Court in which the civil action was pending.

The only difficulty with this hypothesis is that no entry for Field *v.* Lambert has been found in the Minute Book of the Suffolk Inferior Court for the January 1759 term. If the case was in fact decided by that court, either it was omitted from the Minute Book through clerical error, or the questions raised by the plea in abatement on which it was disposed of were decided by the court prior to entry. It is possible that there was some such informal proceeding before the start of the term, established by rule of court to save litigants some of the costs of proceeding in vain cases, but no other evidence of its existence has been uncovered.[13]

In view of these problems, it is possible that the action was brought before a justice of the peace, despite the jurisdictional objections which had seemed to prevail against Field's first action. Lambert, or his counsel, may simply have agreed to waive the jurisdictional questions so that the matter could be disposed of without the expense and delay of a trial in the

---

ince Laws 370. Furthermore, there is no evidence that JA had at this early stage taken steps to procure his admission to practice in any county other than Suffolk.

[11] See Act of 26 June 1699, c. 2, §3, 1 Mass., *Province Laws* 370; Act of 23 April 1743, c. 32, §1, 3 Mass., *Province Laws* 64.

[12] Min. Bk., Inf. Ct., Suffolk, Jan. 1759, No. 100. The suit was on a note. Plaintiff recovered judgment by default of £9 8s. 7d. and costs of £2 7s. 6d. See the writ (in JA's hand and endorsed by him) and the bill of costs in the In-

ferior Court Files, Jan. 1759. Office of the Clerk of the Superior Court for Civil Business, Suffolk County Court House, Boston, Mass.

[13] Under the Act of 15 Jan. 1743, c. 13, §1, 3 Mass., *Province Laws* 29, the jury in the Suffolk County Inferior Court was not to attend until the second Tuesday of each session, in order that pleas in abatement and other nonjury matters might be heard first. No statutory provision for a hearing session prior to the beginning of each term has been found, however. JA's Diary entry, note 18 below, to which the date 29 Dec.

Inferior Court.[14] Or Adams may have convinced his adversaries that in a new proceeding he could successfully argue that the case was within the jurisdiction of a single justice. In October he had made note of authorities from which he might have contended that a justice's court was a court of record.[15] Perhaps he was also prepared to urge that the 40s. limit on the jurisdiction was not exceeded when damages were sought on two separate grounds, each of which alone was within the limit.[16]

In the days following his delivery of the writ, Adams' misgivings continued to mount. He noted endless queries on points of detail in the first and third entries bearing on the case in the Diary Fragment, until, at last exhausted, he asked himself, "What have I been doing. Only drawing a Writt." Finally, Lambert's plea in abatement was filed. The grounds for the plea may have included the failure of the writ to allege Lambert's "addition," or calling, correctly. On this point Adams prepared a fairly elaborate note which is a part of the first *Field v. Lambert* entry in the Diary Fragment. This was probably only preliminary research or thought on the question, but could possibly have been part of an argument. Whether such an argument was ever delivered has not been determined. At length the writ abated, apparently on the different ground that Adams

---

1758 was originally assigned by the editors, would seem to support the preliminary-hearing theory. The position of the entry in the MS is such, however, that it could date from the following week; it is thus also consistent with the clerical-error theory.

[14] Although there was authority in the 18th century that such a waiver of jurisdiction was of no effect if the judgment were later attacked, the rule that the court could raise this question on its own motion seems to have been a more recent development. See Lucking v. Denning, 1 Salk. 201, 202, 91 Eng. Rep. 180, 181 (Q.B. ca. 1702); Mansfield C. & L.M. Ry. Co. v. Swan, 111 U.S. 379 (1884); Shipman, *Common Law Pleading* 385; Dobbs, "The Decline of Jurisdiction by Consent," 40 N.C.L. Rev. 49, 66–75 (1961).

[15] See JA, *Diary and Autobiography,* 1:49, where JA apparently refers to Thomas Wood, *An Institute of the Laws of England* 447 (London, 6th edn., 1738), and Giles Jacob, *A New Law-Dictionary,* title Court (London, 5th edn., 1744), works familiar to him from his studies with Putnam. See JA, *Diary and Autobiography,* 1:173. The passage from Wood, essentially similar to that from Jacob, is as follows: "A Court of *Record* is that which hath Power to

Hold Plea according to the Course of the Common Law, of Real, Personal and Mixt Actions, where the Debt or Damage may be 40s. or Above, and where it may hold Plea of Trespasses *Vi et Armis*; and Whose Acts and Memorials of the Proceedings in the Courts are in Parchment.... A Court *Not of Record* is either, where it cannot hold Plea of Debt or Trespass, if the Debt or Damages amount to 40s. or of Trespasses *Vi et Armis*; or where the Proceedings are not according to the Course of the Common Law, and where the Acts of Court are not Enroll'd in Parchment.... Note, That a Court that is not of Record, cannot impose a Fine, or Imprison." JA also mentioned Michael Dalton, *The Countrey Justice* (London, 1746), undoubtedly referring to this passage at p. 5: "They [i.e. justices of the peace] be called Justices because they be Judges of Record."

[16] In a modern view, at least, if the prior decision in fact had been on jurisdictional grounds, these arguments might have run afoul of the doctrine of res judicata, unless Justice Quincy could be understood to have decided only the question of jurisdiction over the writ before him. See American Law Institute, *Restatement of Judgments* §50 (St. Paul, 1942).

had omitted "the County, in the Direction to the Constables of Braintree," a slip which he had earlier noted in his first list of queries as perhaps constituting "a fatal omission." [17]

The self-doubt apparent in Adams' initial worries about his draftsmanship burst forth again in his reaction to the unfortunate news. He expressed his fears that the affair would make him a laughingstock, then went on to a thorough analysis of his failings:

Impudence, Drollery, Villany, in Lambert, Indiscretion, Inconsideration, Irresolution, and ill Luck in me, and Stinginess as well as ill Luck on the Side of Field, all unnite in this Case to injure me. . . .

Let me Note the fatal Consequences of Precipitation. My first Determination, what to do in this affair was right. I determined not to meddle. But By the cruel Reproaches of my Mother, by the Importunity of Field, and by the fear of having it thought I was incapable of drawing the Writt, I was seduced from that determination, and what is the Consequence? The Writt is defective. It will be said, I undertook the Case but was unable to manage it. This Nonsuit will be in the mouth of every Body. Lambert will proclaim it. . . .

An opinion will spread among the People, that I have not Cunning enough to cope with Lambert. I should endeavor at my first setting out to possess the People with an Opinion of my subtilty and Cunning. But this affair certainly looks like a strong Proof of the Contrary.[18]

Time has proved Adams' fears unfounded, but he seems to have learned at least one lesson that would help him to avoid similar setbacks in the future. "Let me never undertake to draw a Writt," he wrote, "without sufficient Time to examine, and digest in my mind all the Doubts, Queries, Objections that may arise." [19]

That Adams had spent enough time after this writ was drawn in examining "Doubts, Queries, Objections" appears from his many queries concerning it. One group of problems, pertaining to the writ proper, has already been mentioned. They dealt with the defendant's "addition" and the omission of the word "county" from the direction to the constables. These matters would have appeared in the formal part of the writ embodied in the printed portion of the form usually used and so are not found in Adams' draft of the declaration. They seem to have been the only questions actually considered by the court.

A second group of problems concerned the declaration. Adams was worried that many specific allegations were defective. For example, he feared that the words "taken up" were too specific a description of Field's

[17] See JA, *Diary and Autobiography*, 1:65. The "direction" was the phrase at the beginning of the statutory form of writ, "to the sheriffe or marshal of our county of S., his undersheriffe or deputy, greeting." Act of 3 June 1701, c. 2, §1, 1 Mass., *Province Laws* 460 (Inferior Court); Act of 5 June 1701, c. 4, same, p. 462 (Justice of the peace). Where the amount sued for in the Inferior Court was less than £10, writs might "be also directed to the constable of the town." Act of 26 June 1699, c. 2, §3, same, p. 370. A direction to the constable was also proper in a writ to a justice of the peace. Act of 18 June 1697, c. 8, §1, same, p. 282.

[18] JA, *Diary and Autobiography*, 1:64–65.

[19] Same, p. 65.

discovery of the horses and thus might lead to a fatal variance between pleading and proof; that "Damage feasant" was too vague an allegation of the activities of the horses prior to Field's attempt to impound them; that the damage done by the horses should have been pleaded specially; and that whether the forfeiture was to the poor of the precinct or of the town should have been specified.

A more fundamental difficulty lay in Adams' confusion as to whether the action should have been in debt or in trespass. The action of debt lay for the recovery of a sum certain and was the usual form of proceeding for a penalty recoverable by statute. Such actions were usually "qui tam" in form—that is, brought by a private individual "who sues as well in behalf of" whoever was beneficiary of the penalty "as for himself." Trespass, on the other hand, was the proper remedy for damages occasioned by the defendant's direct physical act against the person, property, or lands of the plaintiff. Perhaps Adams may be forgiven his confusion: the statute provided both a fixed penalty, such as was commonly sued for in debt, and actual damages of the sort for which trespass might have been said to lie.

If it was necessary to choose between the two forms, debt probably would have been the better alternative. Recovery of the forfeiture to the poor in trespass does not seem in accord with the direct-injury-damages rationale of that action as it was known in the 18th century. Recovery of the actual damages in debt, on the other hand, seems easier to rationalize, on the theory that the damages, equally with the forfeiture, were owing by virtue of the statute. Contemporary Massachusetts forms and later authority suggest that debt's requirement of a sum certain was relaxed in such statutory actions.[20] Perhaps still another course would have been wiser. If the statute could have been read to permit it, Adams might have brought separate actions of debt for the forfeiture and trespass on the case for the damages. This method, which avoids the conceptual difficulties presented by a single action, was adopted in a revision of the statute enacted in 1789.[21]

Many, if not most, of Adams' "Doubts, Queries, Objections" probably would have had more force in the realm of speculation than in the reality of the courtroom—especially in a jurisdiction not given to excessive formality in pleading. Nevertheless, they are of interest, showing, as they do, not only the excessive legalism of the new-hatched lawyer, but also the painful

[20] See forms attributed to JA's contemporaries, Richard Dana, Jeremiah Gridley, and William Pynchon in *American Precedents of Declarations* 342–344 (N.Y., 2d edn., John Anthon, 1810); compare Reed *v.* Davis, 8 Pick. (Mass.) 514, 516 (1829).

[21] Act of 14 Feb. 1789, §6, 1 Laws of Mass. 458 (1807). See Melody *v.* Reab, 4 Mass. 471, 473 (1808). Trespass on the case, rather than trespass, presum- ably would have been the proper form, because loss of compensation for the harm done by the horses was only an in-direct result of the rescue. Of course, if a separate action could be brought for the damages, the only reasons for bring-ing the forfeiture action at all would seem to be either the desire to lower the town poor rates by providing an addi-tional source of funds, or an urge for revenge upon the defendant.

doubts which can assail even an experienced practitioner who has just concocted pleadings that are slightly out of the ordinary.

◁{22}▷   [THE CASE OF FIELD *v.* LAMBERT, DECEMBER 1758.]

The Mistery of Masonry not Freemasonry, comprehends the Plaistering of Walls and Cielings, as well as the Laying of Bricks and building Chimneys, so that it is more extensive than the Addition of Bricklayer.[1] Masonry deals in Cement, in every Thing which requires the Use of the Trowell, and was an Art, an Occupation before the society that goes by that name was ever heard of in the World, for this society took its Name from that Trade by reason of The Trowell which was an Instrument common to these Gentlemen and their less honourable breth[r]en, the Bricklayers, and Mortar managers. This Society has been called [Lobronorum?], ficto nomine, generosa, compacta societas,[2] which shews it was a Nick name borrowed from these manual Artificers and applied to that Society.

Q[uery]. Is not the omission of the County, in the Direction to the Constables of Braintree, a fatal omission.

2. Should ⟨it⟩ I not have ⟨been⟩ added, after "said Joseph," these Words, "who sues as well in Behalf of the Poor of the North Precinct, in Braintree, as for him self."

3. Would not the Word "found" have been more proper than "taken up" and if Defendant pleads not guilty modo et forma, will not a failure to prove that Field had taken the Horses up i.e. that he had bridled or haltered them or else had begun to drive them towards the Pown,[3] be a failure to prove the Declaration? Or in other Words, will ⟨Evidence⟩ Proof by Witnesses that he had seen the Horses, been to his Neighbours House to borrow a Halter, and then into his own to get a Hand to assist him in catching the Horses, be sufficient Evidence of his taking up the Horses according to the Words of the Declaration.

4. Should there not have been a more express and positive Averrment that the Horses broke into his Close and did Damage the[re] than that which is implied in the Words, "rescu'd 2 Horses which the Plaintiff had taken up Damage feasant,"[4] there?

5. Should it not have been averred, that Lambert entered the Close subtilly and craftily, intending and contriving, to prevent the said Field from driving them to Pound, and of consequence to defraud

Field of his Recompence for the Damages the Horses had done him?

6. The Declaration begins in Trespass, but it concludes in Debt, "which sums so forfeited and due," [5] the Defendant has refused to pay. This sounds like Debt for some certain sum that is compleatly due by force of some Law of the Province. These sums may be said to be compleatly due, but the Damages, that Field was [to] recover for himself, were quite uncertain. Now Q[uery] whether this is not in some sort blending together Debt and Trespass, and Q. whether such a blending is not fatal?

7. It is concluded ad Damnum of said Joseph the whole sum Damages and forfeiture and all.—Q. will not this be fatal.

8. Is Mason a good Addition? [6]

9. Should there not have been a more particular Averment of the Value of the Damages the Horses did, in breaking Fence, trampling and eating Grass &c.

10. What is the Method of Proceedings on an Information? Can an Information be filed vs. Lambert this Court?

11. Should the forfeiture be sett forth to be to the Poor of the North Precinct or to the Poor of the Town of Braintree.

[...] Close against the Road, from which the Horses broke in was [...] in that Place where the Horses broke in [...] Difference, as the Horses had no Right to go in [...] Road? [7]

⁅23⁆ And Q[uery] Whether that Entry and driving away, is a Rescous. Field had not actually taken up the Horses, i.e. had not bridled nor haltered them. [8]

[1] In this passage JA recorded what he had learned from some treatise, not identified but probably a work on Freemasonry, about the origin and application of the name "mason." "Addition" here means the allegation of a party's occupation or degree, which had to be correct or the writ would abate. (See JA, *Legal Papers*, 1:32.) This was a matter of concern to JA in drafting his declaration against Luke Lambert; see Query 8 further on in this entry.

[2] The first word appears to be gibberish. A wild guess is that it may stand for "Laboronorum," in which case the Latin phrase may be tortuously rendered as: "known by the feigned name (ficto nomine) of the noble, federated society of workers"—i.e. Freemasons(?).

[3] Thus apparently in MS; a telescoping of "Town" and "Pound."

[4] Closing quotation mark supplied.

[5] Closing quotation mark supplied.

[6] See note 1, above.

[7] This paragraph falls at the foot of a page, the corner of which has been torn away, taking with it several words in each of the gaps indicated in the text.

[8] The notes on Field *v.* Lambert resume after the following letter to Crawford and its appendage.

[A LETTER TO WILLIAM CRAWFORD TELLING "HOW I LIVE,"
OCTOBER 1758.][1]

To [*William*] Crawford[2]

How it is with you I know not, but if I am rightly informed, I am yet
alive and not dead. And to prove it to you, I will tell you how I live.
I sleep, 12 or 13 Hours, Smoke 10 or 12 Pipes, read 5 or 6 Pages, think
of 19 or 20 Ideas, and eat 3 or 4 Meals, every 24 Hours. I have either
mounted above or sunk below, I have not Penetration enough to say
which, all Thoughts of Fame, Fortune, or even Matrimony. You must
not conclude from all this, that I am in the Vapours. Far otherwise. I
never was in much better Health, or higher Spirits in my Life. Both
my mind and Body are in a very easy situation, tortu[red] with no
Pain, disturbed by no Anxiety, and transported with no Pleasure. The
strongest Desire I have left, is that of seeing my frie[nds] at Worcester,
⟨But when or how that desire will be gratified, I know not.⟩ and the
only Passion I have left, is Envy of the Pleasure You enjoy in living so
near B.G.[3]—Remind the Dr. and his Lady[4] of my sincere friendship,
Mr. Putnam and his Lady,[5] [Col. Gardiner] and his Lady[6] of the same
and Betsy Green, of the sighs, Wishes, Hart Ach, Hopes, Fears, that in
spig[ht] of the vain Boast of stoical Tranqui[li]ty, above expressed,
continually attend the Remembrance of her.

[Pr]ay let me know ⟨e'er long⟩ with[in] this 12 months, whether you
live, as I am at this present Writing, and whether you remember me,
or not. Oh Lethe, either Spare my friends, or drown me and my friends
together, for I will not bear to entertain a fruitless Remembrance of
them, after they have quite forgotten me.—Adieu, write to me, as soon
as you [can?].   J.A.

Contemptu Famæ, contemni Virtutem.[7] A Contempt of Fame
generally begets or accompanies a Contempt of Virtue.—Iago makes
the Reflection, that Fame is but breath, but vibrated Air, an empty
sound. And I believe Persons of his Character, are most inclined to
feel and express such an Indifference about fame.

Crooked Richard says all men alike to some loved Vice incline, Great
men choose greater sins—Ambitions mine![8] Some such Reflections and
Excuses, I suppose, the worst men always make to justify, or palliate to
them selves and others, their own worst Actions. Making such a Reflection is throwing Conscience a bone to pick.

Iago. Reputation is an idle and false Imposition, of[t] got without
Merit and lost without deserving.

[1] No clue as to the date of this letter is furnished by its position among the entries relating to the case of Field *v.* Lambert, because the order in which those entries were written is very uncertain. However, the general tone of the letter, with its many references to Worcester friends, suggests that it was written reasonably soon after JA had moved from Worcester to Braintree early in Oct. 1758 and before the second letter to Crawford, p. 99, below.

[2] William Crawford (1730–1776), College of New Jersey 1755, A.M. Harvard 1761, preached in Worcester and vicinity in the summer of 1756, kept school there in 1758 (see note 4, below), and served as chaplain and surgeon in Wolfe's campaign against Quebec in the following year. Thereafter he practiced medicine in Worcester but finally settled at Fort Pownall on the Penobscot in Maine as chaplain, surgeon, and schoolmaster. (JA, *Diary and Autobiography*, 1:10, 33, 37, 43–44; Sibley-Shipton, *Harvard Graduates*, 13:561–563.)

[3] These initials are helpfully filled out by JA below. "Betsy" was probably Elizabeth (b. 1736), daughter of Col. Thomas and Elizabeth (Church) Greene, of Bristol, R.I., whose family JA had visited in 1757 when he carried dispatches during the siege of Fort William Henry. This Betsy Greene was a sister of Hannah (Greene) Chandler (1734–1765), wife of Col. Gardiner Chandler of Worcester, mentioned immediately below. See JA, *Diary and Autobiography*, 3:268, and references in note 6, below.

[4] Presumably Dr. Nahum Willard (1722–1792) and his wife, the former Elizabeth Townsend, of Bolton. JA boarded with the Willards at the cost of the town when he first kept the school in Worcester (JA, *Diary and Autobiography*, 1:9; 3:263–264). In 1758, probably at the time this letter was written, Crawford "taught the village school, and boarded at Dr. Willard's, '47½ weeks at 6 shillings a week'" (D. Hamilton Hurd, *History of Worcester County, Massachusetts*, Phila., 1889, 2:1554–1555).

[5] James Putnam (1726–1789), Harvard 1746, married Elizabeth Chandler, of Worcester, in 1754. Putnam had settled in Worcester in 1749 and "for twenty years ... had no trained competitor in the practice of law." It was under Putnam's tutelage that JA read law from 1756 to 1758. Even though he was later called "the best lawyer of North America" by Joseph Willard, JA had reservations about Putnam's abilities. See Sibley-Shipton, *Harvard Graduates*, 12:57–64; JA, *Diary and Autobiography*, 1:5 and *passim*; 3:264–272; William Lincoln, *History of Worcester, Massachusetts*, Worcester, 1837, p. 227–228.

[6] MS apparently reads: "C Gadr. and his Lady." Without much question JA is referring to Col. Gardiner Chandler (1723–1782) and his wife, the former Hannah Greene. Chandler was selectman and treasurer of Worcester and JA's closest friend among the numerous and influential Chandler clan in that town. A sister of the Colonel's wife was Betsy Greene, mentioned above and identified in note 3. See JA, *Diary and Autobiography*, 1:2 and *passim*; George Chandler, *The Chandler Family ...*, Boston, 1872, p. 140, 259–263; George S. Greene and Louise B. Clarke, *The Greenes of Rhode Island ...*, New York, 1903, p. 144–145, 241.

[7] Source not identified.

[8] The source of this couplet has not been found. It is not in any of Shakespeare's historical plays nor in Colley Cibber's adaptation of Shakespeare's *Richard III* (1700), although JA's Literary Commonplace Book (M/JA/8, Adams Papers) contains a passage from the Cibber version.

‹{ 24, *upside down* }›

2 Horses—10th. of Octr. 1758. One Pound L.M.

To answer J[oseph] F[ield] &c. in a Plea of Trespass, for that the said Luke [*Lambert*], at Braintree aforesaid, on the 10th of last Octr. with Force and Arms entered the said Joseph's Close there, and there and then with force and Arms drove away and rescued from the said Joseph Two Horses which the said Joseph had taken up in his Close aforesaid, Damage Feasant, and was about to drive to the public Pound in said Braintree, which Rescous is against the Law of the Province, made in the Tenth Year of the Reign of William the 3rd, intituled an Act for Providing of Pounds and to prevent Rescous and Pound Breach, whereby amongst other Things it is enacted, That if any Person shall rescue any Horses, taken up damage feasant, out of [the] Hands of a Person being about to drive them to the Pound; whereby the Party injured may be liable to lose his Damages and the Law be eluded; the Party so offending shall for such Rescous forfeit and [pay] the sum of 40s. to the Use of the Poor of the Town or Precinct where the offence is committed; besides all just Damages unto the Party injured;[2] and an Action hath arisen to the said Joseph to recover the said 40s. aforesaid forfeiture to the Poor, and the Damages which he the said Joseph hath sustained by the said Rescous which he says is equal to Twenty shillings more of the said Luke, which sums so forfeited and due, the said ⟨George⟩ Luke, tho often requested, hath not paid nor either of them, but unjustly refuses to do it, to the Damage of the said Joseph as he saith Three Pounds.

[1] This entry is a partial draft of the declaration in the case of Field *v.* Lambert; see the Editorial Note on this case, p. 82–89, and references there.

In the MS, page ‹{ 24 }› was at one time folded over or placed on the outside of the Diary Fragment when the document was folded laterally and stored. Two results were serious fading of the text at the creases and tears along the edges. The lateral folding exposed a small interval of blank space below the draft of the declaration and its revision (second entry below), and it is in this space that the two notes about the authorship were written in the 19th century, the first attributing the Diary Fragment to Royall Tyler, and the sec-ond disclaiming his authorship. These docketing notes are quoted in the Introduction, p. 7.

[2] Act of 10 June 1698, c. 6, §4, 1 Mass., *Province Laws* 323: "[I]f any person or persons shall rescue any swine, neat cattle, horses or sheep taken up as aforesaid [i.e. "found damage-feasant in any corn-field or other in-closure" (same, §2)], out of the hands of the haward or other person being about to drive them to the pound, where-by the party injured may be liable to loose his damages, and the law be eluded, the party so offending shall for such rescous forfeit and pay the sum of forty shillings to the use of the poor of the town or precinct where the offense is

committed, besides all just damages unto the party injured; to be recovered by action, bill, plaint or information in any of his majesty's courts of record."

[ON INDIGENCE AT HOME, DECEMBER 1758.]

haud facile emergunt quorum Virtutibus obstat
res angusta domi.

They will hardly emerge from Obscurity, whose Virtues are obstruct[ed] by Indigence at home. To whose Virtues, a narrow Thing at home opposes.[1]

[1] This brief entry is written in a very fine hand just above the middle of ⟨24⟩ and is largely obscured by the two more or less continuous parts of JA's draft declaration, which so crowd it from above and below as nearly to efface it. Placed as it is at the center of his struggle over his very first case as a professional lawyer, this tag from Juvenal (*Satire* III, lines 164–165) had an obvious appeal for JA and may be considered a cry from the heart.

[THE CASE OF FIELD *v.* LAMBERT, CONTINUED, DECEMBER 1758.][1]

For that the said Luke, on the 10th of Octr. last, ⟨at⟩ with force and Arms ⟨and against⟩ entered the said Josephs Close ⟨there⟩ in Braintree aforesaid, and then and there with force and Arms drove away, and rescued from the said Joseph tho the said Joseph then and there [...][2] Two Horses which the said Joseph had taken up in his Close aforesaid Damage Feasant, and was about to drive to the public Pound in said Braintree, which Rescous [is] against our Peace and the Law of this Province, made in the Tenth Year of [the Reign of] William the 3d.

[Am?] I sensible of the Importance of the Hazard, I run? I risque my Chara[cter] and of Consequence my Business, on the fate of this Writt. [I am?] in doubt about the sufficiency of it. I am in doubt whether Tresp[ass will] lie upon that Act. Whether the Damages done by the Horses to Fields fences and Grass should not have been more Specially sett forth? Whether it is right to declare, for the forfeiture to the Poor ad damnum of Field. It was desi[rable?] that somebody should sue for that forfeiture, and who so proper as the Party injured. How could Debt have been laid for his Damages, when it is disputable how much they amounted to? The Act says just Damages, but the Act has not [asserted?] how much is just Damage in this Case. But may not Debt lie, [where trespass lies?] Can Damages be given and [assessed?] by a Jury in Debt.

If one declares in an Action of Trespass for the taking away of his Cattle, or one particular Thing, he ought to say, that he took away his Cattle or other Thing Prætii so much. [I] have not declared for taking away the Horses pretii so much, but I have declared that Field sustained so much damage by the Rescous and by the Trespass of the Horses. But if he declares for taking away Things without Life, he ought to say ad Valentiam so much.

Damages are frequently given to the Party and a fine to the King in Trespass. W[hy] then may not damages be recovered to Field and the forfeiture to the Poor in Trespass? In all Trespass there must be a voluntary Act and also a Damage, otherwise Trespass [will?] not lie. Lamberts Entry and driving his Horses were voluntary Acts, and the Damage to Field was the Breach of his fence and destroy[ing] his Grass and [...] his [...].

⊰24, *right side up*⊱ [I declared?] ad Dampnum of Field. How could I have expressed ad dampnum of him and the Poor too.

⊰25⊱ Q[uery]. Whether Debt is not a more proper Action than Trespass?

Should not the Damages the Horses did to the Fences, Grass &c. have been Specially shewn, als.[3] how can Defendant make his Defence.

Does not this Declaration shift from Trespass into Debt?

Can Defendant know without a Special Shewing of the Damage done by the Horses to the Fences, Grass &c., how to combat the Plaintiff, what Evidence to produce.

That heterogeneous Mixture of Debt and Trespass, still perplexes me.

Trespass, Entry, Rescous, ⟨*forfeiture*⟩. Can a Forfeiture be demanded by Plaintiff in Right of another, in an Action for Trespass.

Trespass for Damages, and Debt for forfeiture to the Poor.

Upon the Commission of that Offence, the forfeiture becomes compleatly due to the Poor.—Should not something have been said of his suing in Behalf of the Poor, for the forfeiture.

What have I been doing. Only drawing a Writt.

When a particular Act of the Province is declared on should that Passage of it which is particularly to the Purpose be shewn in hæc Verba.

95

¹ The first paragraph of this entry is evidently a redraft of a part of the declaration begun in the entry next but one above. See Editorial Note on Field *v.* Lambert, p. 82–89, above. Being on the crease of the MS, the text is badly worn.
² Seven or eight words illegible.
³ Alias, i.e. otherwise.

⊰{ *26, upside down* }⊱

[A LIST OF PLEADINGS, OCTOBER–DECEMBER 1758.]¹

Bond to give Deed.

† Trespass on the Case vs. Sherriff for the Default of his Deputy.

† Case by Baron and feme vs. Executor, on a Promise made to the feme while [sole? . . . later?].

† Ind[ebitatus] Ass[umpsit] for service done at a customary Price. Plea, in abatement, that the service was insufficient.

Ind. Ass. for keeping a Horse to Hay. 3.

Sci[re] fa[cias] vs. Bail. 4.

If it was a [. . .] Writ, I'd lay a Quant[um] Mer[uit] as much as he deserved. Can Book be sworn to on Q.M.

Ind. Ass. on a Note of Hand.

† Debt to the Clerk of the Company. On Province Law.

⟨*Trespass on the Case, by an Infant*⟩

Quantum Valebant for Cyder sold by Infant, suing by his father, his guardian [or] next friend.

Trespass for breaking a C[ows leg?]. 6.

† Trespass upon the Case for refusing Marriage after Promise. 7.

† [Trespass upon the Case] on a protested Order vs. Drawer.

† [Trespass upon the Case] for not Building a good Barn according to Order.

Covenant broken, for not warranting Land, according to Cov.

Trespass. Quare Clausum fregit. 9.

Trover and Conversion of a Kettle belonging to Executor.

Partition. 10.

Trespass Q.C.F. & D.f.² 10.

[Wr]it, for declaring at a Bargain unruly Oxen to be orderly. 10.

[Qua]nt. Mer. and Ind. Ass. 2 Counts, for Work and service. 11.

Debt [. . .] by Farmer of Excise qui tam for selling Rum without Licence.

Trespass on the Case by 2d. Indorser vs. 1st Indorser for the original Drawer his [. . .] Absence from the Province and 2d. Indorser unable to pay the Debt. 13.

Trespass on the Case for Breach of Promise of Marriage. 14.

Ejectment vs. Disseisor.

Joindre of Ind. Ass. and Insimul Comp[utassent].

Case by Guardian to non Compos for Labour done by non Compos. ⟨*Money lent sued for by Administrator.*⟩ 16.

Case for Money received to Plaintiff by a [demand?] for Money lent. 16.

Case on a Note for 24 Gallons of Rum. 16.

Ejectment of a Mortgagor by Mortgagee.

Account by Administrator de bonis non vs. Administrator of the Administrator of him to whom the 1st Administration was committed.

Case on an Order accepted and payed by Plaintiff at Defendants Request 18.

[Case] on a Bill protested or refused to be accepted. 18.

Case vs. a Carrier for suffering Goods to be spoiled. 18.

Warrantia Chartæ vs. Heir at law. 19.

Debt vs. Executor for not exhibiting a ful Inventory. 19.

Town Treasurer vs. a Person for entertaining a Tenant without giving Notice to select men, whereby Charge arose to the Town. 20.

⟨*Town Treasurer vs.*⟩

Case ⟨*vs. Town Treasurer*⟩ by Town Treasurer vs. Constable 20.

Case for Bail vs. Principal for Security. 21.

[Case] on an order accepted by Defendant.

Debt for Rent. 21.

⊲{25, *upside down*}⊳ [Trespa]ss on the Case, for not rendring an Account of Oxen received to kill and [sell?].

Warrant to Constable to convey a Pauper to next Town.

[Presen]tment ⟨*vs.... Officer?*⟩ 22.

[Pres]entment for a Riot. 23.

Presentment, for Administering an Oath without Authority.

Complaint, by Farmer of Excise, vs. one for not giving an Account of distilled Liquors and Lemons taken in and sold.

Case, for Mony had and received to Plaintiffs Use. 24

Case by surviving Creditor. 24.

Debt on a Judgment of Court. 25.

Presentment for selling fat, instead of Butter. 25.

Debt, by Town Treasurer vs. a Person for receiving and entertaining a Pauper. 26.

Complaint to a Justice, vs. one for writing scandalous Words, and Warrant thereon 27.

Action for scandalous Words. 28.

Case vs. Defendant for taking away his Son from Plaintiff with whom he lived to learn his Trade, before the Time agreed on was out. 28.

Trover of a Pice of Timber.

[Equity?] of Redemption in a Mortgage Deed. 29.

Debt vs. one for not maintaining his half of a Partition fence, between him and Plaintiff, on 10th of Wm. 3. Chapt. 18.

Case, for not maintaining &c. on the same Law. 29.

⟨Ejectment⟩

Trespass and Ejectment, by Plaintiff [Heir?] to Devisor after Estate T[ail?] ended. 29.

Ejectment. 30.

Trespass on the Case for drowning Plaintiffs Meadow by a Mill dam. 30.

Ejectment. Declaration on Plaintiffs own seizin &c. 30.

Complaint to Justice, vs. Dear Killer. 31.

[...], Caption of a Petition to Gen. Court. 31.

Imparlance, Prayer for one. 32. in Ejectment.

Warrant of Town Treasurer vs. Collector. 32.

¹ This entry, begun on ⟨26⟩ upside down and continued on ⟨25⟩ upside down, apparently comprises a list of pleadings which JA may have copied from another lawyer's pleadings book or book of forms, such as JA himself later compiled, with his law clerks participating. See JA, *Legal Papers*, 1:26–86. The daggers prefixed to certain items may possibly indicate pleadings that JA copied or intended to copy in full.

There is nothing to indicate when the list was compiled. This and the following entry, on Probate Law, are the only ones in the Diary Fragment for which an argument might be made that they belong to JA's period of law study in Worcester, Aug. 1756–Sept. 1758. On the other hand, nothing else in the entire MS suggests that he even had it in his possession in Worcester, and the manner in which these two entries are fitted in among the materials known to date from late 1758 is against their having been written at any other time.

² That is, "Quare Clausum Fregit et Damnum fecit" (*or* "and Damage feasant"?).

[NOTES ON PROBATE LAW, OCTOBER–DECEMBER 1758.]¹

Tis absurd, ⟨to⟩ for a Testator to say, after he has devised his Lands to one in fee, that they shall go over to another.

There is no [Remainder?] to an Estate in fee. A fee simple, upon fee [...] but a Testator may very legally and sensibly devise Lands to one in fee, and then say, in Case Death or any other Accident should happen to incapacitate the Devisee to take, then the Lands shall go to another.

If a Testator should devise £20 to one, and all the Rest of his personal Estate to another, and it should happen that this particular Legacy could not pass to that Legatee, the Residuary Legatee shall have that £20, before the Executor.

¹ These notes, perhaps drawn from a treatise, appear on ⁅ 25 ⁆ of the MS up-side down (i.e. running the same way with the preceding entry) and crowded into a blank space to the right of the later items in the preceding entry. They were thus written later than the list of plead-ings that comprise that entry; see note 1 there.

⁅ 27, *upside down* ⁆
[A LETTER TO WILLIAM CRAWFORD, DESCRIBING A VISIT TO BOSTON, OCTOBER–NOVEMBER 1758.]¹

Mr. Crawford.

Am returned from Boston, and according to my Promise ⟨sett down⟩ begining to write you a Discription or a History of what I saw, and heard, &c.

I distrust my Capacity, without an Invocation, but am afraid to make one, for I know the Muses are not fond of such Work. Take it then in the plain Language of common sense.

My Eyes were entertained with Objects, in every figure and Colour of Deformity, from the Blacksmith in his darksome Shop to the Chim-ney Sweeper rambling in the Streets. My Ears were ravished with every actual or imaginable sound, except harmonious sounds, from the Hurley burley upon Change, to the Rattling and Grumbling of Coaches and Carts &c. The fragrance of the Streets, were a continual feast to my Nostrils.—Thus Pleasure entered all my senses, and roused in my Imagination, scenes of still greater tumult, Discord, Deformity, and filth.²

As for Reason, what Entertainment could that find, among these Crouds? None.

Thus you see the whole Man, the Senses, Imagination and Reason were all, equally, pleased. Was I not happy?

But all this is the dark side.—In reward of this Pain, I had the Pleasure to sit and hear the greatest Lawyers, orators, in short the greatest men, in America, harranging at the Bar, and on the Bench. I had the Pleasure of Spending my Evenings with my friends in the ⟨silent⟩ Joys of serene sedate Conversation, and perhaps it is worth my while to add, I had the Pleasure of seeing a great many, and of feeling some very [pretty?]³ Girls.

¹ The date of this draft letter to Craw-ford has been discussed in the Introduc-tion, p. 14, above, where the conjecture is made that it was written soon after JA's visit to Boston of 24–26 Oct. 1758, when he interviewed leaders of the bar to arrange for his admission, sat in court as an observer, and attended an assembly in "the most Spacious and elegant Room" where were present "the gayest Com-pany of Gentlemen and the finest Row of Ladies, that ever I saw" (*Diary and Autobiography*, 1:54). There were some public festivities in Boston on 24 Oct. to mark "the Return of His Excellency Major-General AMHERST from Al-

bany to this Town" (*Boston Weekly Advertiser*, 30 Oct. 1758, p. 2, col. 1), but the newspapers give few details, having lavished them on the anniversary of the coronation of George II, celebrated on the preceding day.

² Compare the passage in the published *Diary*, 18 [i.e. 19] March 1759,

on "the Rattle Gabble" of the Boston streets, with echoes of Pope's *Imitations of Horace* (*Diary and Autobiography*, 1:80–81).

³ This word is almost entirely worn away in the margin of the MS. The editors' insertion is the merest guess.

◄{ 27, *right side up* }►

[FURTHER NOTES ON CIVIL LAW,
DECEMBER 1758–JANUARY 1759.]¹

Judicial [stipulations] are those which proceed from the mere Office of a Judge, as Surety vs. fraud [...] pursuing a servant, who is in flight. Surety concerning fraud is required, when the Danger is, lest an Adversary commit a fraud [upon things of?] ours. Surety concerning pursuing a servant, is that [when?] an Heir promises the Legatary, that he will pursue at his own Expense a servant [which?] is [given?] as a Legacy, who is running away, and restore either servant or his Value. Prætorial Cautions are those which proceed from the mere Office of the Prætor, as a surety of Damage, that is [...] and of Legacies. Damage is all Diminution of our [Pa]trimony. A Damage not done, is that which is not yet done but which we fear will be done. [A] surety of a Damage, not done, is that by which, the owner of decayed Buildings engages to his Neighbor [that] he will repay thereafter what ever Loss or Damage shall [happen?] by the fault of his buildings. [A] surety of Legacies is that by which the Heir, having given Bondsmen, engages to a Legatary to whom a Legacy [is] bequeathed on Condition, or at a certain day, that he on the fulfilment of the Condition, or [...] of the day, will pay the Legacy [...].² But if the owner will not give the said sureties to the Neighbor, nor the Heir to the Legatary, the Neighbour is put into possession of the decayed House by the Prætor and the Legatary into [possession?] of the hereditary Things. It is peculiar to the Pretors Cau[tions] to [need Bondsmen?]. Convent[ion]al Cautions are those which are conceived by the Agreement [of] either Party. There are as many Kinds of these as there are of things to be contracted. Common are those which proceed as well, from the Office of Prætor, as of that [of] Judge, as that the Estate of a Pupill shall be safe, which is given by Tutors; and a Surety, by which, he who manages the Business of another when he doubts of a Command, he engageing that the Master shall have [...]³ due. Of useless Stipulations. An useless stipulation is one that has no Effect in Law. Stipulations are useless, either by Reason of the Thing, or of the fact included in the Stipulation, or by Reason of the Contractor, or by Reason of the form or manner of the Contract. A stipulation is useless by Reason of the Thing, if any one stipulate a Thing, which neither is, nor can be, in the nature of Things; allso a Thing which is not in Commerce, as a Thing sacred, holy, religious, public, a free man, or at least beyond the Commerce of the stipulator. Also if any one stipulate a property purely, or [even?] the Thing plainly incertain. If any one shall promise the ⟨fact⟩ Act of another, without any Penalty annexed, also [anything that?] is impossible, either in nature or Morals. By Reason of the Contract, if they are unqualified, as dumb, deaf, mad, infant; also, as made between a father and a son or servant and Master; also if any one shall stipulate to Another than himself unless it shall [be] to him to whom it is [. . .], or a Penalty [is annexed?].

Let me get a clear Knowledge of the Proceedings in the Courts of Probate.[4] Ex[ecuto]r, who accepts the Trust is accountable to the Judge of Probate. [A Jud]ge of Probate, by Warrant under his Hand and seal, directed to sherriff &c. to cause such suspected Person to be apprehended, and brought before such Judge to be [examined?] and proceeded with. A Person suspected of convaying or imbezzling Part any Part of the Estate of any Person deceased, shall have been cited, pursuant to Law [*sentence unfinished*]

[1] This entry is a continuation, without break, of JA's notes on Van Muyden's *Tractatio* on Justinian's *Institutes*, entered physically at a much earlier point in the Diary Fragment; see p. 55–59, above, and editorial notes there. The present jottings are based on Van Muyden, p. 121–124, continuing the *Institutes*, bk. 3, title 19, and covering part of title 20.

[2] Three or four words illegible.

[3] Three words illegible.

[4] Although there is no indication of a break in the MS, JA has here obviously dropped Van Muyden. The following three sentences are partly quoted and partly paraphrased from An Act for Further Regulating the Proceedings of the Courts of Probate within this Province, passed by the General Court on 5 Jan. 1753 (Mass., *Province Laws*, 3:639–640).

⊰{ 28 }⊱

[SHAKESPEARE'S CHARACTERS AND FIGURATIVE LANGUAGE, OCTOBER–DECEMBER 1758.][1]

Shakespeare, in the Character of Lady Mackbeth, and of Gertrude, the Wife of old Hamlet, and afterwards of King Claudius, and in the Character of Lady Anne in King Richard, has shewn a sense of the Weakness of Woman's Reason, and strength of their Passions.

The Horror of both divine and Human Vengeance, that attends guilty minds is strongly represented in the Characters of Mackbeth and his Lady. He grows daily more and more timorous of the Nobility, and of every man of [Respect?] in their Realm. At last, they are afraid that the stones and trees, and Birds will reveal their Murder and demand Revenge. Blo[o]d for Blood.

Shakespears vicious Characters are aggravated beyond Life. He draws Ingratitude, Treason, Hypocrisy, Murder, in the strongest Colours of Horror.—In Thinking of any Thing, every Image that can resemble it, rises at once in strong Colours in Shakespears mind. When the News of his Ladies death is brought to Mackbeth, he turns his Thoughts upon Life.

> Out out brief Candle!
> Lifes but a walking Shadow, a Poor Player
> That struts and frets his Hour upon the Stage
> And then is heard no more! It is a Tale
> Told by an Ideot, full of Sound and Fury
> Signifying Nothing.[2]

Here he compares Life, 1st to a Candle, then to a Shadow, an Image taken from scripture, then to a Player on the stage of Life. Now to a Tale told by an Ideot, another scripture similitude.—Persons in Mackbeths situation are very apt to make these Reflections and Comparisons. After having committed every Vice and folly, in order to attain the Goods of this Life, they find that these Goods are all Trifles, light vain, idle Toys, and then they compair Life to such Things with great Wisdom. Oh the Horror and despair, the Distress and Anguish of a guilty mind.

Richard, Claudius, Mackbeth and his Wife and Iago are Characters of Fiends, not of men. The times have been, that when the Brains were out, the man would die, and there an End, but now they rise again with 20 mortal murders on their Crowns, and push us from our stools. Malcolm and Donalbain when they find their father murthered and a bloody Dagger laid near their Bed, and their own Hands stained with Blood, concluded that the Design was to charge the Murder on them, and to avoid the consequences they fled to England, and a faulcon towering in her Pride of Place, was by a mousing Owl haukt at and killed. The faulcon is Duncan, the mousing Owl is Mackbeth. The old man observed the Omen. Rosse takes Notice of another Omen that preceded Duncans Death. Duncans Horses, beauteous and swift, the Minions of their Race, turned wild in Nature, broke their stalls, flung out, contending gainst Obedience, as they would make War with man. Thriftless Ambition that will raven up thy own lifes means.

Mackbeth kills the others that lay in the K[ing]'s Chamber out of pretended Rage at their [Murder] of the King and tells the Lords and Attendants, their faces and Hands were besmeared in blood and that [an] unwiped Dagger laid by the Bed side. Not only Omens preceded, but sympathy in Nature attended Duncans Death. Chimneys were blown down.

> Lamentings heard i'the air, strange screams of Death.
> Of dire Combustion and confusd Events
> New hatchd to the woeful time.
> The obscure bird clamourd the livelong night
> Some say the Earth was feverous and did shake.[3]

Mackbeths Imagination was [struck?] and afraid, was as lively and teemed with Notions, a Thousand thoughts came into his Head when he was [*remainder missing*]

His imagination created 100 things, a Voice crying, Sleep no more, Mackbeth doth Murder Sleep; the innocent Sleep. Sleep is the Idea now. What Thoughts does this call up. Sleep that knits up the ravelled sleeve of Care, the Death of each days Life. As Death is to a mans whole Life, so is ⟨Sleep to a day⟩ each nights Sleep to us, sore Labours Bath, Bath of Labour, Balm of Hurt minds, great natures second Course, chief Nourisher in Lifes feast. The Eye of [*remainder missing*]

[1] There is nothing to indicate the date of these comments on Shakespeare, although it may be noted that on 5? Dec. 1758 JA entered in his *Diary* as published in 1961 an injunction to himself beginning: "Let me search for the Clue, which Led great Shakespeare into the Labyrinth of mental Nature!" (*Diary and Autobiography*, 1:61). As usual, JA's quotations are approximate.

[2] Act V, scene v, lines 23–28.

[3] Act II, scene iii, lines 61, 63–66.

⊰{ *28, upside down* }⊱

[ON A PETITION FROM BRAINTREE TROOPS ENLISTED FOR THE EXPEDITION AGAINST CANADA, DECEMBER 1758–JANUARY 1759.][1]

The general Court agreed to raise 7000 men, to cooperate with his Majesties Forces, for the Reduction of Canada. Agreed, consented by a Vote an Order not by a Law an Act.[2] They make Acts to raise money and clothe the soldiers when raised. But the K[ing], in the british Constitution, and of Consequence the Governor in ours, has the sole Direction of Peace and War. Inlisting men, sending them out, proclaiming War, negociating Peace, concluding Peace, are all with the sovereign's Power. But the Parliament must raise supplies.

The Court direct and impower the Treasurer to borrow £28,000, and they enact that the said £28,000 when[soever] borrowed, shall be issued by the Governor, with Advice of Council, for the levying and cloathing the said 7000 men, pursuant to the Order of this Court, and for no other use.—By Order of Court, and with Advice of Councill.[3]

Cur [*i.e.* Court?] will grant these Petitions, that People may be encouraged to list next Spring, even after the time limited for Inlistments, when the officers are impowered to impress, and not to be so obstinate as some were last Spring. Some refused to the last to inlist, and were dragged into the Service at last. If Money was issued by the Governor to the Officers of this Company or Regiment, to be given as a Bounty to these men, who inlisted after the 2d of May as well as to those before, and the Officers have [defrauded?] them of it, should not this Petition [represent?] the fraud and pray an Order on the officers to make Satisfaction?[4]—Is the Governor, or Coll. Lincoln or Coll. Quincy or Captain Bracket[5] to blame in this Affair. If there was an Order of the Generall Court that such as should inlist after the 2d of May should have the Bounty, as well as those who inlisted before, and the Governor [paid?] Money accordingly, one of them is to blame.

[1] From evidence set forth in note 4, below, the latest possible date that this, physically the last entry in the Diary Fragment, could have been written was the first week or so in Jan. 1759. It was probably written in Dec. 1758, when, as we must suppose, JA was called on to help draft the petition from Joseph Nightingale and others of Braintree that is the subject of these notes.

[2] The General Court on 11 March 1758 "*Voted*, That Seven Thousand Men, inclusive of Officers be raised on the part of this Government, by inlistment for the Intended Expedition against Canada, to be formed into Regiments, and Officer'd by such of the Inhabitants of this Province as His Excellency the Capt. General shall be pleased to appoint: The said Men to be continued in the service for a time not exceeding the first Day of November next, and to be dismissed as much sooner as his Majesty's Service will admit" (Mass., *Province Laws*, 16:153).

This force was recruited to join the army under Gen. James Abercromby at Albany which in the summer of 1758 undertook an amphibious assault on the French stronghold of Fort Carillon (later Fort Ticonderoga) in order to clear the way to Canada. Abercromby's army of 15,000 suffered a disastrous defeat at the hands of Montcalm with a much smaller force. The remains of some of the "inland fleet" in which the British and colonial troops had ascended Lake George were being recovered for reconstruction and preservation in the summer of 1965. See Edward P. Hamilton, *The French and Indian Wars*, N.Y., 1962; *New York Times*, 27 June 1965, p. 1, 55.

[3] JA is here abstracting an Act of 25 March 1758 (Mass., *Province Laws*, 4:76).

[4] On 17 March 1758 the General Court had voted "That each able bodied effective Man who shall voluntarily inlist himself into the intended Expedition against Canada before the fifteenth day of April next shall be intitled to Thirty shillings and upon his passing Muster shall receive a good Blanket and Fifty shillings more for furnishing himself with Cloaths" (same, 16:160). On 21 April—eloquent testimony on how recruiting was progressing—the time for enlistment "upon the same Bounty" was extended until 2 May (same, p. 176).

Among those who failed to meet the later date but enlisted soon afterward in order to avoid being "dragged into the Service at last" by officers with power to impress, was a neighbor of JA's named Joseph Nightingale; see JA, *Diary and*

Autobiography, 1:303. On 10 Jan. 1759 the House of Representatives received and considered the following petition, which JA is discussing here and had presumably helped Nightingale draft:

"A Petition of *Joseph Nightingale,* and others, of *Braintree,* ... praying, that they may be allowed the Bounty voted for those that should inlist into the Service the last Year, for the Expedition against *Canada* before the 2d Day of *May* last, they having inlisted into said Service within a very few Days after the Time assigned, and marched to *Fort-Edward* by Direction of their proper Officers, and served faithfully during the whole Campaign.

"Read and *Ordered,* That this Petition be dismiss'd." (Mass., *House Jour.,* 35:158.)

The original of the Braintree petition has not been found in M-Ar.

[5] Col. Benjamin Lincoln (Sr.), of Hingham (the father of Dr. Bela Lincoln, mentioned frequently above), and Col. Josiah Quincy and Capt. Richard Brackett of Braintree, the principal local militia officers.

Index

Index

This Index has been compiled on the principles set forth in the notes that precede Indexes to previously published volumes in *The Adams Papers*. Readers should perhaps be reminded that references in the form of *"See* (or *See also*) Adams Genealogy" are to a compilation, as yet unpublished, which is described above at p. xviii.

Index

Townsend, Elizabeth. *See* Willard, Mrs. Nahum

Treaties: treaty of amity and commerce with Netherlands (1782), 17–18; provisional articles and definitive treaty of peace with Great Britain (1782–1783), 18, 21, 24; commercial treaties with Barbary States (1784), 26

Trespass: action of, 83–88, 90, 93–95; in list of pleadings, 96–98

Tufts, Dr. Cotton (1732–1815, uncle and cousin of AA, *see* Adams Genealogy): left in charge of the Adamses' affairs in Braintree, 26, 28; helps the Adamses buy the Old House, 30

Tullius, Tully. *See* Cicero

Tupper, Professor Frederick, ed. *Grandmother Tyler's Book*, 27, 30–31

Tyler, Royall (1724–1771, father of the dramatist): sketch of, 22; mentioned, 18

Tyler, Mrs. Royall (Mary Steel, d. 1800, mother of the dramatist), 18, 22, 28

Tyler, Royall (1757–1826, christened William Clark Tyler), the dramatist: biographical account of, 22–30 (*see also* Adams Genealogy); papers of, in Vt. Hist. Soc., ix, xiv, 2, 7, 16, 30–32, illustrated following 42; JA's earliest diary attributed to, 7, 93; AA's account of, 18–25; courts AA2, 18–27, 30; law clerk in Francis Dana's office, 18, 22–23; sets up law office in Braintree, 18, 20; allowed by AA to use JA's legal papers and books, 19–20, 25–26, 28; borrows MS of JA's earliest diary, 19–20; law practice in Falmouth, Maine, 20, 24; buys Borland farm in Braintree, 20, 25, 28, 30; early literary productions of, 20–21, 22, 29; JA's view of his romance with AA2, 20–26; in Revolution, 22; called before Harvard faculty for misconduct (1777), 23; illegitimate son attributed to, 23; admitted to bar, 23; to collect legal debts owed to JA, 26; broken engagement with AA2, 26–27, 29; miniature portrait given to AA2, 27; gives up lodgings at Cranches and moves to Boston, 28, 30; Lincoln's aide-de-camp during Shaysite disturbances, 28–29; his comedy, *The Contrast*, 29, 30; marries Mary Palmer,

30; death, 30; materials gathered for biography of, 31; fate of AA2's correspondence with, 32

Tyler, Mrs. Royall (Mary Palmer, 1775–1866, *see* Adams Genealogy): *Grandmother Tyler's Book: The Recollections of Mary Palmer Tyler*, 27, 28, 30–31; courtship and marriage, 30

Tyler, Rev. Thomas Pickman, unpublished "Memoirs" of Royall Tyler, 22, 28, 31

Tyler Collection, Vt. Hist. Soc., xiv, 2, 16, 22, 30–31, illustrated following 42

United States. *See* Continental Congress; Treaties

Utrecht, Netherlands, xii

Van Muyden. *See* Muyden, Johannes van

Vassall-Borland house. *See* JA, Residences; Adams National Historic Site

Velocity, Winthrop's comments on, 61

Venus, transit of, x

Vermont, 7, 28, 30

Vermont Historical Society: gift of Tyler Coll. to, ix, xiv, 31; JA's earliest diary found in Royall Tyler Coll., 2, 32

Vinnius, Arnoldus, *Institutionum Justiniani commentarius*, 11. *See also* Justinian, *Institutes*

Virgil (Publius Virgilius Maro): *Aeneid*, 68; mentioned, xiii, 73, 78

Virginia, Cornwallis' army in, 17

Warner, Mr., wounded by love, 68

Warrant of contempt, in Field *v.* Lambert, 83–84

Washeba, John, 4

Waterhouse, Dr. Benjamin, 35, 43

Watermarks, "Arms of England," 4, 6

Watertown, Mass.: "great Bridge" over Charles River, 48; mentioned, 33

Weather observations and records, 7–8, 16, 33–35, 43–53

Webb, Nathan (JA's cousin, 1734–1760, *see* Adams Genealogy), 9, 37

Wedge, theory of the, 63

Wentworth, John (1737–1820), later Sir John: sketch of, 67; correspondence with JA partly lost, 67; mentioned, 39

  Letter: From JA (in 1758): discussed, 10–11; text of, 64–65

119

❡ The *Earliest Diary of John Adams* was composed on the Linotype and printed directly from type by the Harvard University Printing Office. Rudolph Ruzicka's *Fairfield Medium*, with several variant characters designed expressly for *The Adams Papers*, is used throughout. The text is set in the eleven-point size and the lines are spaced one and one-half points. The photolithographic illustrations are the work of The Meriden Gravure Company. The cover fabric is a product of the Holliston Mills, Inc., and the books were bound by the Stanhope Bindery. The paper, made by the S. D. Warren Company, is a new grade named *University Text*. It was developed by Harvard University Press, for first use in *The Adams Papers*, and bears its mark. The books were designed by P. J. Conkwright and Burton L. Stratton.